HEADLINE SERIES

No. 312   FOREIGN POLICY ASSOCIATION   Fall

Taiwan Faces
the Twenty-first Century:
Continuing the 'Miracle'

by Steven M. Goldstein

Prologue 3

1   Second Chance on Taiwan:
    Political Reform 10

2   Taiwan's Economic Miracle:
    The Challenges of Success 25

3   Relations Across the Taiwan Strait
    and U.S. Foreign Policy 38

4   Conclusion 62

    Talking It Over 79

    Reading List 80

Cover Design: Ed Bohon $5.95

LIBRARY
COLBY-SAWYER COLLEGE
NEW LONDON, NH 03257

#38464727

The Author

STEVEN M. GOLDSTEIN, professor of government at Smith College, is a graduate of Tufts University and holds a Ph.D. from Columbia University. He taught at Columbia before joining the Smith faculty in 1968.

Goldstein has written widely on questions relating to Chinese foreign policy, domestic politics and revolutionary history. He has lived in Taiwan and Hong Kong and in 1996 he worked with CNN during the presidential elections on Taiwan. He is currently a member of the editorial board of *The China Quarterly* and *The Journal of Contemporary China*.

The author thanks the Chiang Ching-kuo Foundation for its support and Nancy Hearst for her editorial assistance.

The Foreign Policy Association

HEADLINE SERIES (ISSN 0017-8780) is published four times a year, Spring, Summer, Fall and Winter, by the Foreign Policy Association, Inc., 470 Park Avenue So., New York, NY 10016. Chairman, Paul B. Ford; President, Noel V. Lateef; Editor in Chief, Nancy Hoepli-Phalon; Senior Editors, Ann R. Monjo and K.M. Rohan; Assistant Editor, Nicholas Barratt. Subscription rates, $20.00 for 4 issues; $35.00 for 8 issues; $50.00 for 12 issues. Single copy price $5.95; double issue $11.25. Discount 25% on 10 to 99 copies; 30% on 100 to 499; 35% on 500 and over. Payment must accompany all orders. Postage and handling: $2.50 for first copy; $.50 each additional copy. Second-class postage paid at New York, NY, and additional mailing offices. POSTMASTER: Send address changes to HEADLINE SERIES, Foreign Policy Association, 470 Park Avenue So., New York, NY 10016. Copyright 1997 by Foreign Policy Association, Inc. Design by K.M. Rohan. Printed at Science Press, Ephrata, Pennsylvania. Fall 1995. Published June 1997.

Library of Congress Catalog Card No. 97-60819
ISBN 0-87124-176-5

Prologue

Taiwan's current ruling party, the Kuomintang (KMT) or Nationalist party, has roots deep in China's twentieth-century revolution. This historic association has been the single most important influence on the evolution of Taiwan's contemporary politics and foreign policy. As is so often the case in politics, the past weighs heavily on the present.

Failed Revolution on the Mainland

Sun Yat-sen, the KMT's founder (known in Taiwan as the *kuo-fu* or "father of the country"), provided the ideological and institutional foundation for the island's political system. In the early years of the twentieth century, Sun's attempts to overthrow the ruling Qing (Manchu) dynasty were consistent failures, largely because of his movement's shallow roots among the people and its organizational weaknesses. Still, Sun's stature as the symbol of China's revolution grew despite these failures.

The Foreign Policy Association gratefully acknowledges The Freeman Foundation's support for this issue of the HEADLINE SERIES.

3

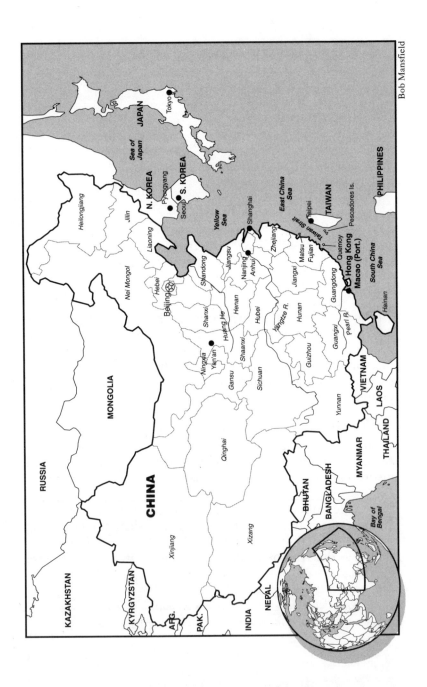

Bob Mansfield

In 1911, when the revolution that would overthrow the dynasty began, Sun was traveling in the American West and could take little credit for the realization of his lifetime ambition. Still, his standing was such that he was immediately chosen, *in absentia*, president of the new Republic of China, and he founded the Kuomintang party in preparation for anticipated parliamentary elections. However, once more Sun failed. He was outmaneuvered by the political cunning and military power of a former imperial general. Again he fled into exile.

In the early 1920s, while building a revolutionary base in South China, Sun agreed to an alliance with the new Bolshevik government in Russia which was seeking allies to offset the threat from the Western imperialist powers. This connection transformed the KMT. With Soviet guidance, the foundations of a strong military, so important during China's warlord era, were laid. The weaknesses in the party's mass base were addressed as the Chinese Communist party (CCP), instructed by Moscow to ally with the KMT, provided dedicated grassroots activists. Finally, the KMT was transformed along the lines of the Soviet Communist party, redressing the organizational weaknesses that had hampered Sun's political efforts in the past. With power concentrated in a few institutions at the center, the Kuomintang, like the Soviet Communist party, was very much a Leninist party.

The ideology that guided the party, however, was not Leninist. Since the first decade of the twentieth century, Sun had been developing his core ideology, later known as the Three People's Principles *(San-min Chu-yi)*: People's Nationalism, People's Democracy and People's Livelihood. The last of these was the least developed. Although it seemed to point toward land reform and some state ownership of large industries,

---

According to the Shanghai communiqué of 1972 issued by the United States and China, "the government of the People's Republic of China is the sole legal government of China; Taiwan is a province of China." The July 1, 1997, return of Hong Kong to Chinese sovereignty may shift China's focus to the cross-strait relationship.

the economic component of Sun's program remained vague. In its final form, People's Democracy suggested a system of five-branch government, combining Western-style executive, legislative and judicial branches (Yuan) with traditional Chinese institutions intended to supervise the bureaucracy and administer civil-service examinations. Although Sun advocated a broad range of powers for the people, he did recognize that there would have to be a period of political "tutelage" during which the party ruled and prepared the citizenry for its new responsibilities. Nationalism was the most passionately argued of the three principles. By the 1920s, following the overthrow of the Manchus, Sun turned his nationalism against the Western powers, calling for an end to their special political and economic privileges in China.

With a revitalized ideology, a strengthened military and a strong organization with grassroots agitators, Sun was ready to move out of his base in south China and realize his dream of reuniting the nation. This never happened, for he died in 1925 at the age of 59.

After a brief struggle, and amid growing tensions with the Communists, Chiang Kai-shek, a conservative military figure, emerged as the KMT's principal leader. By 1928 Chiang was the leader of a Kuomintang-dominated Republic of China established in Nanking (Nanjing). However, success had come at a price. The top leadership was split; national unity was tenuous under the continued influence of China's more powerful warlords; and after a bitter and bloody confrontation the Communists were purged. The CCP moved into the countryside, where it would continue resistance against the KMT.

'Nanking Decade'

For the Nationalists, the years preceding the Japanese invasion of China on July 7, 1937, are frequently referred to as the "Nanking Decade." Compared with the subsequent periods of the Sino-Japanese War and World War II (1937–45) and the civil war in China (1946–49), this decade provided a relatively calm environment in which the KMT could implement its vi-

A portrait of Sun Yat-sen, founder of the Chinese republic, looms over Chiang Kai-shek, president of the Republic of China on Taiwan, as he holds a rare press conference on the mainland's shelling of Quemoy in 1958.

sion for a new China. Indeed, although this period of Nationalist rule is often overlooked, in contrast to the attention paid to the drama of the war against Japan and the defeat of the KMT in the civil war that followed, many historians consider the three periods to be closely linked. Historians differ sharply, however, on the nature of the connection.

For some students of history, developments in the Nanking Decade demonstrated that the Nationalists created the beginnings of a viable regime. According to this view, a workable government was undermined by the war against Japan, which rendered the KMT unable to resist the Communist onslaught in the postwar years. These analysts stress the accomplishments of that period: strong industrial growth; a national unity unknown since 1911; the foundation of a new national financial system; some reclaiming of rights granted to other countries; and the drafting of a new constitution. The war years, however, brought the devastating effects of the Japanese invasion, which left 15 million to 20 million dead, created a huge refugee population, forced the commitment of vast amounts of funds to the war effort and undermined KMT authority in large parts of the country, allowing the Communist movement to grow. The fall of the KMT was for these experts more a result of external events than of policy failures.

Others draw a quite different conclusion. While recognizing many of the accomplishments noted above, as well as the enormity of the wartime devastation, they highlight the failure of the Nationalists to address basic issues facing China during the decade of relative peace. This school of thought argues that the political institutions remained weak despite the new constitution. Chiang is said to have presided over a system that fostered factionalism at the top, corruption at the middle and lower levels and a generally repressive policy toward the people. This combination of weak institutions and lack of political will left China's principal problem, the poor quality of life in the countryside, untouched. Corruption, repression, an unappealing ideological program that seemed to merge elements of traditional Confucianism with European fascism, and an apparent reluctance to confront a growing Japanese threat all undermined KMT support among China's urban intellectuals. When the war came, these policy fault lines were widened. In short, observers holding this view see in these years the emergence of fatal flaws that would hobble the Nationalist government during the war and contribute to its defeat by the Communists soon thereafter.

During and after World War II, the Kuomintang government benefited from its wartime role as one of the major antifascist powers. Still, the interaction of wartime dislocation and the inherent weaknesses of the party strained China's political and military capacities. By the end of the war, the KMT, despite its formidable military power, proved unable to regain control of the country when confronted by a Communist party that had been rejuvenated, not debilitated, during the war years. The civil war, which had never entirely died out despite the facade of a united front against Japan, was rekindled in 1946. Incoherent and often incompetent leadership both in the government and on the battlefield, a lack of responsiveness to popular needs, growing corruption and the creation of an inflationary spiral that ravaged China made the much better armed KMT no match for Communist forces.

At the end of 1949 the party that only a dozen years earlier had been China's most prominent and vibrant revolutionary force collapsed and the Nationalists were driven off the mainland. As the remnants of Chiang's government regrouped on the island of Taiwan, the ideology, institutions and legacies of the past would continue to shape the contours of the new Kuomintang regime. But this time the outcome would be very different.

1

Second Chance on Taiwan: Political Reform

IT IS NOT unprecedented for political exiles from China to seek refuge on the island of Taiwan, about 100 miles off the nation's southeast coast. In the middle of the seventeenth century, after the Manchus had overthrown the Ming dynasty, an adventurer and supporter of the old dynasty, Koxinga, used the island as a base for resistance. Previous to this time, China's rulers had neglected Taiwan, with its small aboriginal population, leaving it to Western maritime powers. The Portuguese were among the first to arrive, their lasting contribution being a name for the island—*Ilha Formosa* (beautiful isle).

The Dutch, among the last to arrive, were forced off when the Ming loyalists settled. When the Manchus finally defeated them in 1683, Taiwan became an administrative subdivision of Fukien (Fujian), the coastal Chinese province which it faces. For the next two centuries the island remained a backwater. Emigration from the mainland (particularly Fujian) continued, but only in the latter part of the nineteenth century did China's central government show interest in Taiwan. Ties with the mainland ended abruptly when Taiwan was ceded to Japan in 1895 after China's defeat in the Sino-Japanese War. For the next 50 years the island was a colony of Japan.

Chinese who lived on Taiwan after 1895 thus experienced a history different from that of their compatriots on the mainland. While mainlanders lived through the Nationalist revolution, the conflicts between the Communists and the Nationalists and the brutal World War II Japanese invasion, those on Taiwan were subjects of the Japanese emperor, untouched by these events. Japanese rule was harsh at times, but there was none of the barbarism that characterized Japan's occupation of China.

As World War II ended, Chiang Kai-shek's Nationalist government pressed for the recovery of territories lost to the Japanese. At the Cairo, Egypt, conference in November 1943, the United States, Britain and China agreed that Taiwan would be returned to China; the pledge was confirmed by the United States, Britain and the Soviet Union at the Potsdam, Germany, meetings in July 1945, and realized in October of that year when the Japanese garrison surrendered to Nationalist troops. After 50 years of Japanese rule, Taiwan was reincorporated into China.

As Thomas Gold, professor of sociology at the University of California at Berkeley, has argued in his classic study *State and Society in the Taiwan Miracle*, it was not a happy reunion. When Chiang's forces arrived, they had bitter memories of Japanese brutality on the mainland. They mistrusted and resented a population that, though composed of Chinese, seemed sympathetic to Japan. The reimposition of Nationalist rule seemed to many in Taiwan more an occupation by an alien power than a liberation by fellow Chinese. Nationalist officials swarmed onto the island, seizing property and imposing the same kind of corrupt, repressive rule that existed on the mainland. Tensions between islanders and mainlanders erupted into violence after KMT officials sought to arrest a black-market cigarette vendor in Taipei, where the Nationalists established their capital. The so-called 2/28 Incident (February 28, 1947) led the Taiwanese to attempt to create their own administration, which in turn prompted a brutal Nationalist reaction. Troops from the mainland systematically murdered thousands of the island's elite—and potential political opposition. A fundamental cleavage was created between Taiwan's resident Chinese and those Chinese who, in increasing numbers, were being driven from the mainland.

In October 1949, the Communists, in effective control of the mainland, declared the founding of a People's Republic of China (PRC) that included the "province" of Taiwan. By December the remnants of the KMT government of the old Republic of China sought sanctuary on Taiwan and the nearby Pescadores islands, declaring themselves (and not the "rebellious" government in Beijing, the PRC capital) to be the legitimate government of China. In addition, they continued to occupy island groupings which were never considered anything but mainland territory. The most famous of these were Quemoy and Matsu, the "offshore islands" located two and ten miles respectively off the coast of Fujian.

In the months that followed, the Nationalists prepared for a Communist invasion. The confrontation across the Taiwan Strait had begun. It was assumed that this confrontation would not last long. In the spring of 1950, mainland forces were massing to invade Taiwan and it seemed as if President Harry S. Truman and his secretary of state, Dean Acheson, were ready to write off the island and deal with the Communists on the mainland.

However, when North Korea invaded South Korea in June 1950, everything changed. Concurrent with the decision to defend South Korea, the Truman Administration dispatched the U.S. Seventh Fleet to the Taiwan Strait to prevent the spread of the conflict, and by August Congress approved a small amount of American foreign aid for the KMT on Taiwan. When Chinese troops entered the Korean War and engaged American troops in October-November 1950, the U.S. commitment to Taiwan was sealed. Fate had given the Kuomintang a second chance.

Reform and Revival on Taiwan

After the KMT had fled to Taiwan, it continued to frame relations with the mainland in terms of a continuing civil war between two parties claiming the right to rule China. Until his death in 1975, Chiang made the defense of Taiwan from the PRC and the commitment to retake the mainland the center-pieces of government policy. The Kuomintang asserted that its rule on Taiwan was that of a national regime temporarily exiled to one province and mobilized for the military defeat of a domestic enemy in rebellion since the 1930s. These histori-cally based assumptions not only legitimized the KMT's politi-cal dominance but they also conditioned the unique set of political institutions by which it ruled.

These institutions maintained continuity with Sun Yat-sen's political principles and the earlier Kuomintang government on the mainland. The constitution of 1947, which mandated a Legislative Yuan (branch), an indirectly elected president and an Executive Yuan headed by a premier, remained in effect. The exiled representatives held onto their seats after the move to Taiwan and their separation from the mainland constituen-cies they supposedly represented. Despite supplementary elec-tions held on Taiwan in 1969 and 1972, the overwhelming ma-jority of representatives had no political links to Taiwan. Simi-larly, the president was selected by an electoral body (the National Assembly) whose members had been chosen on the mainland.

These tenuous links were largely of symbolic importance, since the formal constitution mattered little. The assumption of continued "Communist rebellion" meant that the suspen-sion of normal constitutional guarantees, first introduced on the mainland and then applied to Taiwan, remained in effect. The real seat of power lay outside the government, in the military and in the Kuomintang dominated by Chiang.

Almost all the major central governmental and military posts were held by KMT mainlanders. The Leninist party organiza-tion sponsored by Sun Yat-sen remained. Like its Communist enemy, the KMT tolerated only a few token opposition parties and used its extensive organizational network to dominate the civilian government as well as the military. In Taipei, as in Beijing, policy was made in party bodies and major government appointments were approved there. Kuomintang China had thus been transplanted from the mainland to Taiwan. The islanders became party to a civil war which they had never experienced. The restrictions on political activity led one former KMT governor of the island to condemn the government as a police state.

Yet one should be careful not to overdo the theme of continuity with mainland rule. Chiang and many of his colleagues seemed to have learned some lessons from their humiliating defeat in 1949. This experience, combined with the pressures exerted by American advisers, conditioned some new policies which eased the burden of KMT rule on the people of Taiwan and smoothed the way toward later democratic evolution.

For example, since the KMT government claimed to be the central government for China, Taiwan maintained a separate provincial government, which encompassed additional layers of local government. While they were largely excluded from the central government and military, Taiwanese were admitted to the KMT and encouraged to participate in elections at the county or municipal level.

In the socioeconomic realm Chiang moved quickly to carry out land reform on Taiwan. This was motivated by a desire to weaken the local landed elite, but it was also reflective of a more liberal view of what the economy should be. Chiang resisted demands from some in his party to limit the private sector. Indeed, during these years this sector not only enjoyed vigorous growth but was dominated by Taiwanese.

An informal division of power thus took root with the former mainlanders (about 15 percent of the island's population) keeping a tight grip on the central politico-military realm, leaving the islanders to participate locally and prosper economically.

Chiang Kai-shek, Kuomintang leader from 1928 until his death in Taiwan in 1975, is shown here with his politically dynamic wife, Soong Mei-ling, and his elder son, Chiang Ching-kuo, the future president of Taiwan (1978 to 1988).

Initiating Democracy: The First Decade of Reform

The initiation of democratic reform in Taiwan during the 1980s was prompted by both domestic and international developments. The major global influences were the gradual weakening of Taiwan-U.S. relations and the island's growing isolation in the international community, which began when it lost its seat at the United Nations in 1971, continued through the visit of President Richard M. Nixon to China the following year and reached its culmination with derecognition by the United States and the end of the bilateral mutual defense treaty in 1979. Any legitimacy that had been based on the KMT's claim to represent all China was eroded and much of the world simply refused to accept the fiction any longer. This change in the international environment was accompanied by problems at home. By the 1980s, the murder of a dissident residing in the United States (which also worsened Taiwan-U.S. relations), a serious financial scandal involving a prominent KMT legislator and the growth of public protests combined with international pressures to force the government to find new bases for legitimization that were rooted less in the claim to represent all China than in a more responsive relationship with the people of Taiwan.

However, these events alone were not enough to bring about change. Most commentators recognize the central role played by President Chiang Ching-kuo, the son of Chiang Kai-shek. He had been sent by his father for training in the Soviet Union during the 1930s and was later associated with brutal KMT repression on the mainland as well as Taiwan. Chiang's subsequent preparation to succeed his father included holding major government positions, among them intelligence and security, as well as minister of defense and premier. During this period he became attuned to the regime's growing crisis of legitimacy.

Chiang Ching-kuo Lifts Martial Law

In the years after his father's death in 1975, Chiang (who finally became president in 1978) showed signs that he was willing to deal with social demands differently than he had earlier. He relaxed—but did not abolish—harsh restrictions on political opposition. This led to the emergence, not without its violent moments, of a Taiwanese opposition movement. In the mid-1980s, Chiang set into motion a reform which would radically transform the political system. The lifting of the 1934 martial law decree in 1987 led to the removal of the military from government, and put an end to many restrictions on public assembly and speech. It also legalized the first true opposition party, the Democratic Progressive party (DPP), which traced its roots to the Taiwanese opposition of the late 1970s.

Within the KMT, Chiang sought more democracy and the inclusion of larger numbers of native Taiwanese. Chiang moved with greater caution, however, in reforming government organizations. He was never able to confront successfully the aging and politically meaningless delegates who continued to dominate the representative bodies of the central government. Although he drafted plans for their retirement, little was accomplished. Still, supplementary elections continued, increasing the islanders' representation, and a historic moment was reached in the 1986 supplementary election to the Legislative Yuan, when the KMT for the first time faced an opposition party, the DPP. Legislative bodies were still unrepresentative of the island's population, however, and Chiang Ching-kuo died in 1988 without having addressed this central issue of constitutional reform.

Chiang's protégé and successor, Lee Teng-hui, was faced with both the consequences and unfinished agenda of his predecessor's program. Born in Taiwan to a well-to-do farming family in 1923, Lee's life parallels that of many of his generation. He received his secondary education in Japanese schools and after World War II attended Kyoto University. His first career was in agronomy, in which field he earned a Ph.D. from Cornell University in the late 1960s. By the 1970s he was in government service. With Chiang Ching-kuo's patronage, he held positions as cabinet minister, mayor of Taipei, provincial governor and finally, in 1984, vice president of Taiwan. Upon Chiang Ching-kuo's death in January 1988, he became president—the first native Taiwanese to hold the office.

Lee may have been Chiang's protégé, but he was deeply distrusted by the mainlanders in the KMT's "old guard." Their unhappiness with Lee's succession stemmed from more than his Taiwanese origins. More important to them was the likelihood that Lee would continue the democratizing reforms of the past. The conservatives believed these would fatally undermine the place of the Kuomintang by exposing it to increasing competition from local elites. Moreover, they resisted holding new elections on Taiwan only, arguing that this would end the party's claim to represent all of China. In their view this would represent a de facto concession of the civil war to the Communists and would undermine a major pillar of the party's legitimacy.

Lee, on the contrary, appeared to calculate that only democratization would assure this legitimacy, and in dealing with his powerful opponents in the KMT he proved to be a more skilled politician than most had anticipated. By mid-1992, he had become party chairman and had been reelected president in his own right by the mainlander-dominated National Assembly. In early 1993, he forced out the mainlander premier, Hau Pei-tsun, a tough representative of the old-style Kuomintang (now called the "nonmainstream" faction) and replaced him with a Taiwanese, Lien Chan, a political ally from the KMT's "mainstream" faction.

The president and premier of Taiwan were now both islanders, a clear indication that the barriers to islander political participation that had been erected in the late 1940s were eroding. Earlier, the repeal of the temporary provisions in 1991, a court decision requiring the dissolution of the old representative bodies and subsequent constitutional amendments all paved the way for the election in 1992 of an entirely new Legislative Yuan chosen only by the people of Taiwan. The fiction of mainland representation was finally ended.

Although the Legislative Yuan was nominally the nation's supreme lawmaking body, its actual power had been weakened by both the dominance of members representing phantom constituencies and the restrictions placed upon its powers by extraconstitutional decrees resulting from the civil war on the mainland. With the 1992 elections and the repeal of these decrees, the Legislative Yuan became a much more assertive body. For the Democratic Progressive party, the legislature became a most important sounding board as well as a primary base from which to check the power of the KMT-dominated Executive Yuan and presidency.

The DPP, which had its roots in the exiled Taiwan independence movement and the *Tang-wai* (outside the party) movement that challenged the Kuomintang during the 1970s, was formally established as an opposition party in 1986. Although it

Taiwan's President Lee Teng-hui delivering a National Day speech on October 10, 1992, the anniversary of the 1911 revolution in China.

campaigned on a platform of democracy and clean government, the party was most closely associated with demands for Taiwan's independence. Most of its leadership, as well as the mass of its supporters, were islanders.

In 1991, on the eve of the elections for a reconstituted National Assembly (a body charged with amending the constitution and, until 1994, electing the president—not to be confused with the lawmaking Legislative Yuan), the DPP platform officially endorsed independence for Taiwan. The party did worse than expected in the National Assembly elections, and before the elections the following year for the Legislative Yuan a more moderate position was taken. In these elections the DPP gained 31 percent of the vote, electing 51 representatives to the 161-member body. In the 1993 elections for county magistrates and city mayors, the party gained 41 percent of the vote, and in 1994 the DPP candidate was elected mayor of Taipei. The DPP was on its way to becoming a major challenger to the KMT.

19

It was not, however, the only challenger. As noted above, the emergence of Lee Teng-hui had divided the KMT. These divisions became clear during the elections of 1992 and were exacerbated by the forced resignation of Hau Pei-tsun. Finally, on the eve of the August 1993 party congress that would confirm Lee's solid control of the party, a group of mainlanders bolted from the KMT and founded the New party (NP). While this party seemed to be appealing to middle-class voters with its focus on the corruption and rigidity resulting from one-party rule, its platform also stressed opposition to independence and more aggressive pursuit of unification with the mainland. The NP achieved status as a legitimate third party when it gained 17 percent of the vote in the constituencies where it fielded candidates in 1993 and, the following year, elected 11 members to the Taipei city council, compared to 20 KMT and 18 DPP members.

By early 1995, the stage seemed set for a decisive year in the evolution of politics on Taiwan. A new election for the Legislative Yuan was scheduled for December. In March 1996, the president would be chosen for the first time by direct popular election, as would the National Assembly. The elections of 1995–96 would thus open "national" offices to election by the island's population and constitute the first tests of Taiwan's new multiparty system.

The elections would also be a decisive stage in the process of lessening the links between the government in Taiwan and its political past on the mainland. The KMT's leaders were no longer veterans of the civil war of the 1930s and 1940s. Taiwan's party system and government were no longer shaped by the political institutions which grew out of that conflict. In the intervening years, the process of attenuation had been so subtle that many on Taiwan might have missed—or were given an excuse for missing—its profound significance. During the elections of 1995–96, the mainland's leaders, who had not forgotten the past, dramatically brought this fact to the forefront of Taiwan's politics.

Since the early 1990s, Beijing had been carefully watching

Taiwan's domestic political development. It viewed with growing concern the democratization process that had ended the KMT dictatorship and made government more accountable to the people of the island. The PRC much preferred to deal with a single party, led by those still tied to their historic origins on the mainland. Now, political institutions rooted in Taiwan were growing and even the Kuomintang was changing its nature. In particular, after 1994 mainland leaders grew increasingly suspicious of Lee Teng-hui, considering him to be a separatist at heart. When in June 1995 Lee returned to his alma mater, Cornell University, in Ithaca, New York, and delivered a speech extolling the "Republic of China on Taiwan," Beijing became convinced that something had to be done in the coming, pivotal year to arrest the perceived growth of separatist sentiment.

During the summer of 1995, Beijing used military exercises, missile firings, hostile rhetoric and an unwillingness to hold

REUTERS Simon Kwong/Archive Photos

More than 10,000 Taiwanese participated in a rally for independent presidential candidate Lin Yang-kang, also supported by the New party, the day before the March 23, 1996, presidential elections.

high-level, unofficial talks with Taiwan as ways of expressing its unhappiness with Lee. As the December 1995 elections to the Legislative Yuan approached, the mainland once again held missile tests and military exercises on the coast, hoping to influence an election that many considered (and might have hoped) would end in a three-party stalemate. Ultimately the big winner was the New party, which won a surprising 13 percent of the vote and 21 seats. The KMT finished with only 46 percent of the popular vote and 85 seats, a slim majority in a legislative body of 164, while the DPP remained constant at 33 percent and 54 seats.

Many commentators attributed the dramatic successes of the more-unificationist New party to the threats from the PRC. Others downplayed the mainland factor, emphasizing the role of NP organization, as well as the potential of a party that could draw disenchanted KMT loyalists and middle-class elements. Indeed, two prominent KMT leaders, Lin Yang-kang and former premier Hau Pei-tsun, announced their independent candidacy for the presidency and vice-presidency respectively and actively campaigned for New party candidates in the legislative elections.

Thus, as the March 1996 elections for the presidency and the National Assembly approached, Beijing's leaders and many in the West believed that mainland actions might be able to arrest the drift toward separation that was accompanying Taiwan's democratization and to reorient Taipei's politics toward the unsettled questions of the past. In the weeks before the elections the PRC acted on this assumption and, indeed, suffered a serious setback.

The contest for president was a four-way race. Lee Teng-hui ran for reelection and chose his premier, Lien Chan, as his running mate. The New party withdrew its candidates and threw its support behind the "independent" ticket of the former KMT leaders, Lin and Hau. The DPP nominated Peng Ming-min, a longtime independence leader, for president and Frank Hsieh, a lawyer, for vice president. Finally, Chen Li-an, the son of a prominent KMT leader, declared as an independent with Wang Ching-feng, the only woman in the race, as his running mate. Significantly, all the presidential candidates except Chen were Taiwanese, and three of the four had impressive KMT backgrounds.

PRC Actions Aid Lee

Initial signs suggested that the campaign, while historic, might also be uninteresting. The PRC was, however, concerned. In its commentaries during the run-up to the elections, Beijing depicted the KMT and the DPP as running on the same independence platform and it seemed to favor the New party. In early March 1996, Beijing decided to express its views by means of missile tests close to the Taiwan coast, and the nature of the election changed. The mainland was clearly warning the United States and the people of Taiwan against Taiwan independence and also, perhaps, seeking to influence a large undecided vote. Domestic political differences between the parties were eclipsed and the focus turned once again to mainland policy.

The mainland's military threat forced both opposition parties to retreat from their earlier policies (a process begun during the previous summer's show of force). The DPP downplayed the need for declaring independence (a call that had been somewhat muted since the 1991 elections), arguing that since Taiwan already was a "sovereign country" it would be unnecessary. The New party muted its calls for unification, advocating a "commonwealth" of equal entities on both sides of the strait. No party wanted to appear to be appeasing or provoking the mainland; all rushed to the center.

Ironically, the PRC's action had apparently tipped the undecided balance in Lee's favor. It was he who could best present himself as a voice of moderation with the experience to deal with the mainland. Voters seemed reluctant to change presidents at this point, and even the supporters of the DPP seemed ready to abandon their candidate to support the president in his defiance of cross-strait threats. In the end, Lee achieved a remarkable victory, garnering 54 percent of the vote, with the DPP winning 21 percent, Lin and Hau 15 percent and Chen and Wang 10 percent. It was the best showing for the KMT since democratization began. However, in the crucial but less mainland-oriented elections for the National Assembly, the pro-Kuomintang message was less clear. The ruling party lost the three-quarters majority needed to amend the constitution, gaining 50 percent of the vote and 183 of 334 seats. The DPP registered 30 percent of the vote with 99 seats and the New party 14 percent of the vote with 46 seats, percentages remarkably similar to the results of the legislative elections.

The elections of 1996 marked an important watershed in Taiwan's transition from a mainland-rooted, single-party authoritarian system to an island-based democratic government. In his victory speech, President Lee claimed that the "gates of democracy are now fully opened." But he was speaking prematurely. There are many issues which must be addressed if the accomplishments of the past are to be consolidated into a viable democratic system.

Yet, continuing political change is only one of the challenges on Taiwan's horizon. Political reform is occurring within the context of two other formidable tasks: the restructuring of the economy and the redefinition of the island's relations with the mainland and the international community.

2

Taiwan's Economic Miracle:
The Challenges of Success

M UCH OF THE STORY of Taiwan's economic transformation can be told simply by statistics. Since 1952 annual economic growth rates have ranged between 6 and 10 percent. In 1952 per capita share of the island's gross national product (GNP) was U.S. $50. In 1996 Taiwan's per capita income ranked among the highest in Asia, U.S. $12,439. Typical of an industrializing society, the basic structure of the economy has shifted dramatically. In 1952 agriculture represented 32 percent of gross domestic product (GDP) and about 95 percent of total exports; by 1996 it had dropped to less than 4 percent of GDP and less than 5 percent of total exports. Industrial production, which had been around 20 percent of GDP and about 5 percent of total exports in 1952, was 36 percent of GDP and over 95 percent of exports in 1996. Making up the remainder of the economic profile was the service sector (banking, real estate, insurance, tourism, trading companies, transportation etc.), with 60 percent of GDP in 1996. In the past four decades,

Taiwan has changed from an agricultural economy to an industrialized one supported by a vibrant service sector.

Clearly exports have played a crucial role in this transformation. Today Taiwan ranks as the world's fourteenth-largest trader, with exports representing almost 43 percent of GNP and foreign-exchange reserves standing at U.S. $90 billion. Economists call such development via foreign trade "export-oriented industrialization" (EOI) and contrast it with "import-substituting industrialization" (ISI), which protects industry from international competition and relies on internal markets.

Recently many economists, joined by the World Bank, have argued that EOI and not ISI is the preferable strategy for late-developing economies. An export policy is said to open up an economy to the world, allowing it to find a niche in the international economy appropriate to its current stage of development. Subjected to the pressure of international competition and benefiting from the growth of global technology, development occurs with greater efficiency and fewer price or foreign-exchange distortions. The result is steady progress up the ladder of the global economy as the domestic economy moves from one based on agriculture to one producing labor-intensive goods and, eventually, technologically sophisticated products.

Economists who agree on the importance of exporting to industrial development are sharply divided over the role that government plays. For some, the role of government in the East Asian economies has been, and should be, one of supporting the free operation of the market. Others contend that the key to success has been the creation of an interventionist state, able to frustrate some, though not all, market mechanisms and so "to get prices wrong" in order to guide the economy in a direction that it might not naturally go. Most who adhere to this view contend that such governments have to be not only competent but also nondemocratic, so as to resist successfully social pressures that might frustrate guidance of the economy. With an authoritarian regime in charge, it is argued, a developing economy is best able to adapt to the challenges and opportunities that a changing global economy presents to those seeking to industrialize via export promotion.

Taiwan's economy has certainly changed its shape in response to domestic and global changes. Scholars who have studied the island's economic development generally agree that since 1949 it has gone through four stages: import substitution during most of the 1950s; export-oriented industrialization, characterized by labor-intensive goods, throughout the 1960s; continuation of export-oriented industrialization from the 1970s into the mid-1980s, characterized by more technologically sophisticated goods and some import substitution; and finally, from the late 1980s until the present, the continuation, within an uncertain domestic and international environment, of the previous period's mix, supplemented by an effort to make Taiwan a "regional operations center" for international businesses in Asia.

Taiwan's Road to Industrialization: 1950s to 1980s

The 50 years as a Japanese colony had contributed to Taiwan's development in ways that would serve the empire and provide a showcase of the benefits that all Asia might gain under Japan. When their rule ended in late 1945, the Japanese left behind a disciplined and educated work force as well as a small entrepreneurial class. However, for the most part, five decades of Japanese dominance had prevented the emergence of either a politically active society or one in which there existed powerful classes (such as landowners) who might have resisted land reform and the shift to industrialization. Japanese rule dominated not only the politics and society of the island but also its economy. The major sinews of economic power such as banking, manufacturing and utilities were monopolies controlled by a foreign government.

Given the priorities and capabilities that the KMT brought from the mainland, the Japanese legacy was essential to the party's success in establishing its political rule on the island and beginning the process of economic rebirth. Taiwan had, in the first place, a society over which authoritarian rule could be easily established, particularly since the brutality of the 2/28 Incident. This control, at first considered necessary in the wake of the defeat on the mainland, would later be essential for effective state intervention in the economy. Of course, this authoritarian rule was facilitated by more than the nature of the Taiwanese people. Despite all its faults, the KMT government came to the island with certain advantages. First among these was great size; it has been referred to as "a continental-sized administration," with capabilities far greater than were needed to govern Taiwan.

In addition to its large size, much that the KMT brought from the mainland was useful. The philosophy of Sun Yat-sen recognized the importance of state control over large sectors of the economy, and on the mainland the Nationalist government had developed planning bodies and policies that, thanks to the state-dominated economy left on Taiwan by the Japanese, could be quickly put into place. The government also came with a legacy of failure that many, including Chiang Kai-shek, were determined to escape. Finally, although many went to Hong Kong, large numbers of Shanghai textile manufacturers brought their machinery and production and marketing know-how to the island.

Ironically, the emergence of the cold war in Asia provided a nurturing environment for the early stages of Taiwan's economic miracle. The North Korean invasion of South Korea and the PRC's subsequent intervention led to a decisive change in American policy, providing a military shield for the island. For the remainder of the 1950s, Washington sought to bolster Taiwan, presenting it as a capitalist (and democratic!) contrast with "Red China." The United States was providing not simply military protection but also crucial economic aid and advice.

With American encouragement, the newly established government on Taiwan spent the first decade of its rule pursuing economic recovery through land reform, inflation control and other initiatives. The government limited Taiwan's trading contacts with the rest of the world and fostered a manufacturing sector that could produce much of what was needed domestically. This was, of course, a classic example of import substitution, and it made some sense given the uncertain nature of the economy in Taiwan and the rest of the world.

Significant U.S. Assistance

It was in this first decade of KMT rule on Taiwan that American aid proved most important. U.S. assistance during these years represented about 6 percent of the island's GNP and supplied roughly 40 percent of gross investment. Besides granting a large amount of military aid, Washington provided manufacturing equipment, raw materials and consumer goods. While this level of aid assured that U.S. advisers would be listened to, the orientation of the economy was not determined solely by them.

From the outset, planning had been an integral part of the KMT's conception of its role. The government played an essential part in the orientation of the economy. It did so through planning bodies (which included American advisers) that sought to identify where new development would be most appropriate; by the use of import controls and foreign-exchange allocation; and, most importantly, through the establishment of state-owned enterprises in crucial sectors such as mining, utilities and textiles. These large state-owned sectors represented almost half of all industrial production.

By the end of the 1950s, the limits of import substitution were becoming apparent. Taiwan was a small island with a finite domestic market and few raw materials. After nearly a decade, imports had been restricted to the point where 10 percent of Taiwan's consumer goods were imported. However, the domestic market was becoming saturated; manufacturers were suffering from excessive competition, leading to bankruptcies. The government was also becoming sensitive to the growth of political corruption as bureaucratic decisions on foreign exchange and credit became matters of life and death for the business community.

Besides these classic deficiencies of import substitution, other external factors were affecting Taiwan's economic decisionmakers. An apparently serious invasion threat from the mainland in 1958 brought with it strong American military support and also the caution that Washington would not tolerate any attempts by Taiwan to "recover" (i.e., invade) the mainland. In addition, Taipei was informed that the substantial economic aid provided in the past would be phased out, and that it would have to rely more heavily on its own policies and resources to develop the island's economy. By the early 1960s Taiwan moved into its first phase of export-oriented industrialization. The "economic miracle" had begun.

In terms of global economics, the shift came at a propitious time. The 1960s were years of expansive economic growth and relatively little protectionism in the developed countries. Moreover, many Western industrialized nations, as well as Japan, were looking for offshore locations where they might move product lines that were becoming less profitable at home because of rising labor costs.

Many local entrepreneurs became partners in foreign corporations. Others went into business for themselves, producing a wide variety of goods in enterprises ranging from large workshops to substantial factories. These businesses, mostly family-run and owned by islanders, produced clothing and footwear which were either marketed abroad or were made to foreign specifications. Increasingly, these small firms began to produce component parts for foreign-owned assembly plants. Throughout the 1960s, manufacturing's share of GNP continued to grow, and Taiwan's exports expanded by almost 30 percent a year.

Those who see economic success as the result of allowing the market to do its work without government intervention interpret this story as a vindication of their views. Taiwan, they argue, succeeded because the government got out of the business of economic management and allowed its people to exploit their comparative advantage in cheap labor within the international economy. Others see it differently. Robert Wade of the University of Sussex, England, argues that these years saw the emergence of a "governed market" in Taiwan, whereby government administration supplemented and sometimes supplanted the free market.

Wade and others point to the crucial role that the economic bureaucracy played in providing an environment hospitable to foreign investment and, further, in structuring that investment and guiding it into areas most beneficial to the island. In the famous case of the establishment of a Singer sewing machine company in Taiwan, for example, the government insisted that an increasing percentage of components be manufactured locally rather than imported.

Moreover, although exports were promoted, some analysts have stressed that free trade was not. The government continued to restrict imports, using tariffs and licenses to protect a growing and increasingly sophisticated industrial sector at home while applying lower rates and tariff rebates on materials imported for use in export production. Through its total control of the banking system, the economic bureaucracy provided preferential rates for loans to exporters or to those who would seek entry into certain export markets. By political repression and control of labor unions, the government slowed the growth of wages and maintained the labor discipline so appreciated by foreign investors. Finally, the continued prominence of state-owned enterprises in such areas as utilities and manufacturing (steel and chemicals for synthetic fabrics and plastics) allowed regulation of the private economy through control of prices and availability.

The Precarious Seventies

The 1970s were the years of oil crises, inflation, exchange-rate fluctuations and general uncertainty in the world markets that not only rendered sources of raw materials unreliable but also raised questions regarding the viability of markets for Taiwan's exports. Moreover, the expansive world trade climate of the 1960s was contracting as developed countries became more protectionist at home and less tolerant of protectionism abroad. America's failure in the Vietnam War, the visit of President Nixon to Beijing and Taiwan's loss of its seat in the UN in

1971–72 all highlighted a fragile security situation. Finally, the inexorable rise of wages in Taiwan combined with the emergence of new sources of low-cost labor in the Third World to add even more urgency to the need for an economic adjustment.

In response to these issues Taiwan sought to move out of labor-intensive production and into the manufacture of more sophisticated products. It also diversified industrial production in order to serve the home market, providing domestic sources of production materials for export industries, meeting some of Taiwan's military needs and tapping the island's increasingly affluent population to replace some of the market share lost abroad. This process has been described as secondary import substitution. During the second half of the 1970s, the island was producing materials and component parts for its own manufacturing needs, especially in export industries, and thus was relying less on foreign sources. Specifically, the island was able to produce artificial fibers, chemicals, machinery, iron and steel for its own use in producing exportable products.

The success of these adjustments is clear from UN statistics compiled by Bela Balassa:

Exports (in %)	1963	1973	1981	1988
Food and live animals	54.7	13.3	9.2	7.4
Industrial manufactures	18.4	83.4	88.4	91.2
of which				
Textile, apparel, leather	9.3	31.5	28.3	22.7
Chemicals	2.0	8.7	9.7	10.3
Engineering products	1.1	26.2	33.1	43.7

In the first stages of export-oriented industrialization, Taiwan was still exporting primarily agricultural goods and, within industrial manufactures, labor-intensive apparel took the lead. Over the next 25 years, industrial manufactures increased their share dramatically, and within that sector there was a clear shift away from labor-intensive wearing apparel toward engineering products, especially items such as radio and television sets and, increasingly, computer-related equipment. Higher wages were justified in these upscale products, particularly as the rate of automation rose.

For a decade beginning in the mid-1970s, Taiwan's economy underwent a series of successful and dramatic adjustments to the changing opportunities and dangers in the global economy. In the view of most economists, these adjustments were not the result of natural market forces at work; once again the role of the state was prominent. The government relied in large part on its old repertoire of tools: control of credit, tax relief, import restrictions and a very large increase in the role of state enterprises, which took the lead in producing import-substituting products. Economists point to the development of the crucial high-technology sector of the economy as an example of the decisive impact of the state, which helped to found research institutions and created incentives as well as production facilities for those ready to enter this new area.

This was a very special kind of state leadership. It was a large, newly reconstituted bureaucracy nestled in an authoritarian state. Many scholars argue that precisely these characteristics made Taiwan's "economic miracle" possible. It was not simply that the bureaucracy had the skills and the tools to shape the economy, but that it was part of a larger government insulated from the demands of the people. This insulation permitted actions ranging from shifts in production orientation that damaged the interests of those previously successful to efforts to maintain a welcoming investment environment through the suppression of both wages and union activity.

By the late 1980s, Taiwan's government underwent a fundamental change. Constitutional reform and social activism were challenging the autonomous nature of the state. In the view of many observers, changes were afoot that would decisively affect the speed, consistency and integrity with which the government could make economic policy. At the same time the problems of adaptation to a radically changing international economy were not abating; indeed, in many ways they were intensifying. Could a democratizing government in Taiwan meet these challenges and continue the island's "economic miracle"?

The Economic Challenges of the 1990s and Beyond

The changing international environment since the late 1980s has affected Taiwan in many ways. Some, such as rising labor costs, resentments caused by the island's favorable trade balance and scrutiny of trade practices, are not totally new. These issues have, however, developed within the context of a newer set of challenges resulting from the growing importance of a global system of trade, first under the aegis of the General Agreement on Tariffs and Trade (GATT), formed in 1948 to reduce trade barriers, and subsequently under its more structured successor, the World Trade Organization (WTO), which took over from GATT in 1995. Many of the practices that fueled Taiwan's past economic growth will no longer be tolerated under these new regimes.

By the late 1980s, the outline of an economic strategy for the next century was taking shape. In order to meet the challenge of rising labor costs, legislation was passed to allow Taiwanese capital to be invested abroad. This combined with the lifting of sanctions on travel to the mainland to create a virtual flight of labor-intensive industries (plastic notions, footwear, clothing and toys) out of the country in search of cheaper labor on the mainland and in Southeast Asia. Thousands of small companies moved their production lines and managers abroad. Although cultural affinities made the mainland the preferred target of offshore investment, Taiwanese businesses under strong government pressure to "go south" became the largest foreign investors in Vietnam and in the former U.S. naval base at Subic Bay in the Philippines. Impatience with trade imbalances and with protectionist behavior in the West was addressed by moving some production (particularly high-tech) to the more industrialized countries, thus leap-frogging trade barriers, as Japanese car manufacturers had done.

A second component of the strategy was to move aggressively into more technologically sophisticated and profitable

34

Courtesy of Government Information Office, Republic of China

In the Hsinchu industrial park, an important
computer and electronics engineering and manufacturing
center, workers turn out IC chips.

high-tech production. The focus remained on computers and
computer-related products. By the end of 1996 Taiwan had
become the third-largest information products manufacturer in
the world, behind the United States and Japan. It had 95 percent of the world market in hand-held scanners and more than
50 percent of the world market share in items ranging from
motherboards (74 percent) to VGA cards (55 percent) to moni-
tors (50 percent). Finally, with the help of intense cooperation
between the government, the private sector and foreign corporations, Taiwan has sought to generate its own technological
breakthroughs.

Despite the fact that these new hi-tech export lines were
prospering, Taiwan announced a plan designed to add a third
facet to the island's involvement in the international economic
system. Seeking to exploit its geographical position, strong industrial base, growing service sector and the niche that might

35

be created by Hong Kong's return to mainland control, the government announced plans to make the island an Asia-Pacific Regional Operations Center. It would serve as an operations center in three areas: as a transportation hub through which trade, by air or sea, with the rest of Asia would pass; as the provider of specialized services for Asia-oriented businesses in sectors such as telecommunications, the media and financial services; and as a production and management center, where foreign companies could establish manufacturing facilities as well as regional offices.

This is an ambitious plan that responds to, and seeks to take advantage of, both the evolving international economy as well as changes in East Asia. It moves Taiwan on a very different trajectory than that of the past. Its success depends on the government's ability to change much of the economic and political structure that has evolved since the 1960s. Bureaucracies will have to be reoriented, aggrieved domestic constituencies managed with care and government structures reshaped. Until these formidable domestic challenges can be met, the plan's realization remains very much in doubt.

Yet, even if these reforms can be accomplished, it still might not be enough. There are external factors restricting Taiwan's development options. The most important of these results from the continuing, and even intensifying, conflict with the mainland. By the early 1990s, the leadership in Beijing had concluded that Taiwan was seeking not merely to widen and deepen its global economic relations, but to use those relations to promote its political position in the world. The mainland began sending a very clear message: it intended to monitor Taiwan's foreign contacts and to oppose any participation in international organizations or bilateral relations that gave the island greater prominence or in any way diminished the mainland's claim to be the central government of the province of Taiwan. Most specifically, Beijing has demanded agreement that Taiwan will not be admitted to the World Trade Organization until the mainland's application has been approved.

Although the mainland has been a large part of the problem

in Taiwan's adapting to its changed economic circumstances, it has also helped provide a solution since Taiwan implemented new regulations allowing travel to the mainland and the export of investment capital. These measures gave new life to industrialists in sectors of the economy facing rising labor costs. Direct investment or transportation links to the mainland are still forbidden, but by investing through Hong Kong entities and transshipping through the former colony, Taiwanese enterprises have established production facilities on the mainland and are bringing semifinished goods back to Taiwan for final export. These "sunset industries" have prospered on the mainland and are being followed to the PRC by others more technologically advanced. By the mid-1990s, only investment from Hong Kong and Macao was growing faster than that from Taiwan, estimated at U.S. $20 billion to U.S. $30 billion. Cross-strait trade totaling about U.S. $22 billion was running overwhelmingly (over six to one) in favor of Taiwan's exports. The mainland-oriented sector of the economy, dependent on stable cross-strait relations, has become an important growth area for Taiwan.

Good relations with the mainland will be essential to the success of the plan for a regional operations center. The mainland is generally viewed as the next economic giant in Asia. Unless Taiwan can establish stable direct shipping and air links with the mainland, it cannot be considered a significant transportation hub. Moreover, even with such links, it would make no sense for any corporation to locate a regional headquarters on the island or partake of its financial facilities if relations across the strait are severely strained. Indeed, for many, perhaps most, global corporations, expressions of Beijing's unhappiness with such relocations or the danger of cross-strait conflict, such as that which developed in 1995–96, would be a deterrent to moving to Taiwan. In short, relations with the mainland represent not simply a security issue for the island, as has been the case in the past. Proper management of cross-strait relations is vital to Taiwan's economic future.

3

Relations Across the Taiwan Strait and U.S. Foreign Policy

IN THE LAST YEARS of the Chinese civil war (1946–49), the KMT received support from the United States at levels which most American military and political leaders considered unjustified. Still, domestic supporters of the Nationalists had to be placated and, more importantly, the emerging cold war required an unpopular military buildup and huge amounts of aid to Europe. Despite these pressures, when the KMT was routed to Taiwan in 1949 and a successful Communist invasion seemed imminent, President Truman was prepared to let the island—and the Nationalists—fall and to deal with the newly established government of the People's Republic of China.

After Chinese "volunteers" joined the Korean War in October 1950, the People's Republic of China (dubbed "Red China"), by then closely allied with the Soviet Union, was depicted as the leading edge of the international Communist movement in Asia. "Free China" was presented as America's brave ally in the Pacific, valiantly resisting yet another threat to world peace. So, with considerable help from the Taiwan lobby in the United States, the mainland was demonized and the KMT government on Taiwan, idealized. During the next two decades, thanks in large part to American efforts, the Nationalist government would become larger than life—or even larger than the island to which it had been exiled.

1950–71: 'Free China' vs. 'Red China'

These efforts were first evident at the UN. Before the Korean War, Washington seemed resigned to the fact that the new Communist government in China would be recognized as a legitimate successor and would take the permanent seat occupied by the Nationalist delegate. When Chinese troops entered the Korean War, however, the diplomatic situation changed. With American prodding, the UN branded the PRC an aggressor nation and declared an economic embargo. The claim of the rump government on Taiwan to be the legitimate government of all China thus received invaluable validation from the keystone international organization of the postwar era.

As the Korean War dragged on, the Truman Administration, under growing domestic political pressure, embellished its depiction of Taiwan as the true government of China and as a fortress of freedom in Asia. Under the Eisenhower Administration (1953–61), with Secretary of State John Foster Dulles setting the tone, the world was pictured as the evil international Communist camp facing the free world. Antipathy to the PRC soon became one of the foundations of America's global posture, and conciliatory gestures from Beijing in the mid-1950s were rebuffed although ambassadorial talks between the two nations had begun in Geneva, Switzerland. By the end of the decade, Soviet-American relations began to thaw, contributing to a growing rift in the Sino-Soviet alliance. Despite the changed American attitude toward the leader of the Soviet bloc, hostility toward Beijing was intensified.

The end result of increased antipathy toward the mainland

was, of course, greater support for Taiwan. The charges by Senator Joseph R. McCarthy (R-Wisc., 1947–57) and others that the KMT was a victim of Communist-engineered American perfidy and not its own incompetence made it politically difficult to slight Taiwan. Washington's pronouncements of support for the Nationalist government's right to represent all China intensified, as did pressure on America's allies to toe the line. In Asia, the Administration, at first hesitant, later acceded to Chiang Kai-shek's urgings to include Taiwan in the growing web of anti-PRC alliances. Although the island was not invited to join the Southeast Asia Treaty Organization (Seato), founded in 1954 following PRC attacks on the Nationalist-held offshore islands, the United States signed a treaty of mutual defense with the KMT government on Taiwan that same year. This was accompanied by massive amounts of military aid. The island that Truman and Acheson had thought expendable was now declared by the President to be "vital to the security of the United States and the free world."

In the Administrations of Presidents John F. Kennedy (1961–63) and Lyndon B. Johnson (1963–69), American policy remained basically the same. Although Kennedy may have considered a shift in policy toward the mainland, actual policy changed very little—if anything, it became more hostile. Under Johnson, while there was continued talk within the Administration of a new China policy and American elite as well as public opinion seemed ready for new initiatives, the demonization of the mainland became even more intense. The reason was obvious. The American involvement in the Vietnam War was being justified in terms of the PRC's military aid to North Vietnam and of opposition to the growth of PRC-encouraged insurgency movements throughout the Third World.

Thus, thanks to a series of international developments tied to the unfolding cold war, the defeated KMT did not slip into that special obscurity reserved for failed political movements. Rather, for two decades it was allowed to conduct foreign policy as if nothing had happened on the mainland during the late 1940s. In the global arena, the Taiwan government was recognized as still holding the political mandate that it had so clearly lost in 1949. In the early 1960s, Taiwan had missions in almost 60 countries. The island enjoyed full membership in the UN and its economic and social organizations.

Implications of U.S. Support for Taiwan

Still, the island's relationship with the United States was clearly the most important element in determining its global standing. Without American intervention, driven by the perceived demands of the cold war, Taiwan would never have been accorded the international recognition it enjoyed. Moreover, the ties with the United States provided other benefits, such as economic and military assistance. Finally, the most important dividend of the relationship was the assurance of protection from mainland attack provided by the mutual security treaty. Under the American umbrella (indeed, there was talk of the use of nuclear weapons to defend Taiwan in 1954–55 and 1958), the island could concentrate on its economic growth.

Yet, despite the rhetoric of a rock-solid alliance, things were not exactly as they seemed. For the United States, maintaining Nationalist power was important less in and of itself than for the message that it sent regarding America's anti-Communist global policy and for the constituencies it placated at home. For Taiwan, of course, the alliance was a matter of life and death. Given the imbalance in the relative importance of the alliance to each country and the overwhelming preponderance of power on Washington's side, one might have expected that successive American Administrations would be able to call the tune. Yet, as the 1954, 1958 and 1962 Taiwan-mainland crises demonstrated, this was not the case. It was very much a give-and-take relationship. In all these instances, Taipei insisted on taking positions that, in Washington's view, threatened to intensify and not reduce tensions in the area. However, the symbolism of Taiwan for global as well as Asian policy and the KMT's vocal political supporters within the United States necessitated care in dealing with the Nationalist regime, even when its policies endangered American interests by threatening to drag the United States into an unwanted conflict with the mainland and/or the Soviet Union.

Chiang Kai-shek seemed to be aware of this fact and manipulated the alliance masterfully. It was not so much that he was committed to the fact of an invasion of the mainland, but rather that he needed to use words and deeds to keep alive the claim of his government to be the legitimate ruler of all China. This claim was the foundation for the KMT's authoritarian rule on Taiwan and allowed the party to reject demands for new elections. Indeed, keeping this claim alive was one of the main goals of Taiwan's foreign policy. And, thanks to American policy, the goal was achieved.

However, in many ways it was a nominal achievement. Although the KMT used international recognition to legitimize its rule at home, most nations made little effort to conceal the fact that they were reluctantly subscribing to a fiction promoted by American policymakers. They would recognize reality as soon as Washington was ready to do so. Throughout the 1960s it was in America's interest, both in Asia and the rest of the world, to maintain this mantle of legitimacy over Taipei. However, the reality of Mao Zedong's government on the mainland was becoming undeniable and the U.S. domestic political mood was shifting.

New Era: U.S. Rapprochement with the Mainland

The announcement in July 1971 that Henry A. Kissinger, President Nixon's national security adviser, had met with Chinese Premier Zhou Enlai in Beijing to arrange a presidential trip to the PRC the following year stunned not only the government on Taiwan but also diplomats throughout the world. Hints of rapprochement had been coming out of both Washington and Beijing since the fall of 1968. The fundamental impulses driving the process toward improved relations included pressing mainland concerns with a growing Soviet threat following the 1968 invasion of Czechoslovakia and the Nixon-Kissinger sense of the importance of a PRC link in dealing with the Soviet Union as well as with a successful American disengagement from Vietnam. The issue of Taiwan was a major stumbling block.

The previous American posture toward Taiwan and the mainland had left the leadership in Beijing deeply suspicious. Their position was simple and remarkably consistent throughout the 1950s and 1960s. Taiwan was a subordinate part of the PRC, to be ruled by the legitimate government in Beijing. The settlement of the differences between the island and the legitimate government of the mainland was an internal matter to be resolved solely between the two parties. The treaties and agreements made by the island were invalid, as were its votes at the UN. In particular, the relationship with the United States constituted an unacceptable "imperialist" interference in China's domestic politics. While Beijing would talk with Washington regarding tensions concerning Taiwan, it would not discuss the island's fate with the United States, nor would it make any pledges to abjure force in the resolution of the issue. Pressure for any such pledge was an illegitimate encroachment on the PRC's sovereignty. The most Beijing would agree to was to seek a peaceful resolution.

When Kissinger arrived in Beijing more than 10 years later, the Politburo laid down three requirements for normalization that resonated with these earlier demands: the United States must recognize the People's Republic of China as the sole legitimate government of China, withdraw its troops from Taiwan and abrogate the 1954 treaty of mutual defense. Kissinger and Nixon knew the domestic political costs of concessions on these issues and knew, too, the impact which a sudden abandonment of Taiwan, close on the heels of the Vietnam debacle, would have on the international image of the United States. Their strategy was to accommodate the mainland's demands, but not to give in to them. Specifically, they sought to put off the Taiwan question and develop Sino-American relations.

After more Kissinger talks and the Nixon visit in February 1972, a formula was devised to permit improved relations to go forward. The American side agreed privately to pursue the issue of mutual recognition during Nixon's second term. In the meanwhile, through a series of parallel statements in the Sino-American Shanghai communiqué of February 1972, each side restated its position. The PRC continued to insist on its earlier position. The United States reiterated "its interest in a peaceful settlement of the Taiwan question by the Chinese themselves" and "affirmed" an "ultimate objective of the withdrawal of all U.S. forces and military installations from Taiwan." Finally, in an attempt to deal with the sovereignty question, there was a unilateral American declaration:

> *The United States acknowledges that all Chinese on either side of the Taiwan Strait maintain there is but one China and that Taiwan is a part of China. The United States government does not challenge that position.*

Diplomatic Isolation

For Taiwan, the developments of 1971–72 were a shock that affected its domestic politics and international relations. The tenuous nature of Taiwan's acceptance in the international community became immediately apparent. The simple fact of the Kissinger visit was enough to end the deadlock at the UN in October 1971. Taiwan was replaced by the PRC. During the next two years, almost half the nations maintaining diplomatic relations with Taiwan switched their recognition to the mainland, resulting in 111 countries recognizing Beijing and only 23, Taipei.

Taiwan made immediate efforts to counter its diplomatic isolation. By the late 1970s, its interaction with the outside world had fallen into a pattern which came to be known as substantive (or virtual) diplomacy—what one might call nonofficial diplomacy. As Ralph Clough of Johns Hopkins University has noted, despite the blows on the formal diplomatic front, unofficial relations with the rest of the world thrived. By the mid-1970s, the island was maintaining trade relations with more than 100 countries and the total volume of foreign trade was continuing to rise dramatically. Through the creation of Taiwanese trade offices abroad and unofficial representations in

Taipei by major trading partners, these ties were strengthened.

Taiwan's relations with the United States were permanently changed after 1971. To be sure, economic relations thrived and even some aid continued. However, from Taipei's perspective, the KMT had been betrayed by the Nixon/Kissinger diplomacy. The drift of Sino-American relations after 1972, despite growing Chinese impatience with the slow pace, made it apparent that full recognition of the mainland was just a matter of time. Although the U.S. embassy remained in Taipei, military ties lessened (fulfilling a Chinese precondition) and a definite chill developed in the relationship. Moreover, the establishment in 1973 of liaison offices (embassies in all but name) in Beijing and Washington reduced the importance of "official" U.S. relations with Taiwan. In December 1978 it was announced that the United States would recognize the PRC and allow the mutual defense treaty with Taiwan to lapse. The announcement caused considerable concern and anger on Taiwan: the Nationalists' staunch ally and primary supporter in the free world had joined those who would no longer maintain the fiction that the KMT represented all of China. However, there was rejoicing in Beijing by China's new reform leadership, headed by Deng Xiaoping.

But when the terms of normalization became entangled with politics in Washington, Beijing became infuriated. Despite an earlier unanimous Senate resolution requesting consultation on any change in relations with the mainland, the White House had proceeded in secret. In response to the normalization agreement, a bipartisan congressional effort radically reformulated a relatively innocuous, Administration-sponsored Taiwan Enabling Act into the Taiwan Relations Act. The latter committed the United States to a broader relationship with and greater commitment to Taiwan than had been discussed in the talks with Beijing.

The congressional legislation made some accommodation to the mainland's concerns by dodging the question of what, in fact, actually was the status of the government on Taiwan. References were made to "the governing authorities on Taiwan," "the people on Taiwan," or just "Taiwan." Apart from these minor concessions, Congress outlined an American policy that provoked Beijing's ire.

(1) It states that it is the "policy of the United States...to make clear" that diplomatic relations with the mainland were based on the "expectation that the future of Taiwan will be determined by peaceful means"; to "consider any effort to determine the future of Taiwan by other than peaceful means, including by boycotts or embargoes, a threat to the peace and security of the western Pacific area and of grave concern to the United States"; to furnish "Taiwan with arms of a defensive character; and to maintain the capacity of the United States to resist" any coercive actions that would jeopardize the security, or the economic or social system of the people on Taiwan.

(2) It recognizes the continued standing of domestic laws and international agreements pertaining to Taiwan, despite the absence of diplomatic relations.

(3) It provides for an embassy-equivalent to be known as The American Institute in Taiwan to be established and staffed by civil-service personnel "separated" temporarily from the government.

(4) It allows for a similar "Taiwan instrumentality" to be established in Washington with the same number of personnel that had served previously, who would enjoy the same privileges.

(5) It mandates congressional oversight of the implementation of the provisions of the act.

Not surprisingly, the Taiwan Relations Act was bitterly denounced by the PRC as a contravention of the terms of normalization. Although it was unclear exactly how binding the statute would be on President Jimmy Carter (1977–81) and his successors, it has remained a major source of continued Chinese distrust. In Beijing's view, the United States was meddling in purely domestic matters and further violating the PRC's sovereignty by mandating quasi-diplomatic relations with—and arms sales to—a subordinate "province" in rebellion. For the Nationalist government the act represented a lifeline of continued support from the nation that had saved it from destruction.

For U.S. policymakers who wanted to extract themselves gradually from the mainland-Taiwan conflict as tensions were reduced, this was very nearly the worst of all possible worlds. Both the PRC and Taiwan saw the United States as very much involved and able to damage their interests in dealings with the other side. Washington's policy thus had to occupy a tenuous middle position, between demands from Beijing to attenuate ties with Taiwan and pressure from Taipei to make them even stronger. Moreover, Presidents after Carter have had to act within the context of a post-cold-war international environment, continued politicization of the cross-strait issue at home and an often erratic relationship with the PRC.

Still, despite a brief crisis during the Reagan Administration over the continued sales of arms to Taiwan, Harry Harding, of George Washington University, was probably right when he noted that by the late 1980s Taiwan had become "a remarkably muted issue in Sino-American relations." Indeed, American officials began to speak openly and supportively of the possibility of "peaceful unification" in the Taiwan Strait.

Impact of Tiananmen

Things changed decisively as a result of the demonstrations in Beijing's Tiananmen Square from April to June 1989 and their aftermath. The PRC leadership condemned the protests as "counterrevolutionary," part of a Western plot to subvert the nation by undermining its political values and institutions. They suspected that American policy toward Taiwan was also part of that plot. On Taiwan, increasingly open domestic politics elicited calls for *de jure* or at least virtual independence from the mainland. Beijing attributed much of this to American encouragement. Such suspicions seemed justified against the background of growing congressional support for Taiwan and Tibet and President George Bush's preelection shift to a more pro-Taiwan policy by selling F-16 fighter jets to Taiwan and supporting Taiwan's independent entry into GATT. Yet, given past good relations with Bush, who had headed the liaison office in Beijing in 1974–75, the response from the mainland was muted.

With the election of Bill Clinton in November 1992, Beijing's suspicions seemed likely to increase. As governor of Arkansas, the President-elect had visited Taiwan four times (including attending Lee Teng-hui's inauguration in 1988), and candidate Clinton had harshly criticized President Bush for his management of relations with the PRC. In his first Administration, President Clinton continued earlier policies toward Taiwan, particularly arms sales and the leasing of naval equipment, permitted cabinet-level trips to Taiwan and approved a change in the name and status of the Taiwan representative's offices in the United States to terms more acceptable to Taipei.

For the most part, however, even as relations with the mainland moved along an erratic track, the U.S. State Department sought to continue to mute the Taiwan question. Washington remained somewhat aloof, repeating previous policy regarding "'one China' and a peaceful resolution." More directly, it continued to show some consideration for mainland sensitivities. In 1993 President Clinton hosted a summit meeting of APEC (Asia-Pacific Economic Cooperation) forum in Seattle, Washington, at which Taiwan's representative was only the minister of economic affairs, Vincent Siew. On his way to Central America in May 1994, President Lee was allowed to make a refueling stop in Honolulu, Hawaii, and, if he wished, to use a VIP lounge in the military base—but not to stay overnight or leave the airport.

In fact, Lee, perhaps seeking to garner sympathy as well as score political points, refused even to leave the plane. Although this was the first time a president of Taiwan was permitted a transit stop in the United States, many in Congress thought Lee had been treated discourteously.

When Cornell University invited Lee to make an address during a reunion visit in the summer of 1995, the State Department refused Lee a visa on the grounds that it might remove an "essential element of unofficiality" in relations with Taiwan. Taipei's public relations machine in Washington went into gear, and a bitterly divided Congress enjoyed a rare moment of bipartisanship, voting 97–1 in the Senate and 360–0 in the House to allow Lee's visit. The trip proved a decisive moment in Taiwan-mainland relations. Beijing, angered by the visit and the perceived political tone of Lee's Cornell speech, saw the trip as a violation of an Administration pledge regarding high-level visits. The PRC denounced the decision, canceling several exchanges with the United States as well as a high-level meeting of cross-strait representatives. It also began a campaign of hostility toward Taiwan that included military threats as well as missile firings, which culminated in the Sino-U.S. cross-strait confrontation during the island's presidential election in March 1996. The train of events that began in the summer of 1995 marked a sea change in Taiwan's relations with the mainland.

The fact that this shift was occasioned by American policy— and condemned by Beijing— demonstrates a somewhat contradictory point. The sharp mainland reaction to the Lee visit was as much a response to the drift of post-1979 mainland-Taiwan relations as it was to the actions of a divided American government. In contrast to the 1950s and 1960s, much more than American policy was influencing cross-strait relations. Since 1978 the domestic politics and international policies of Beijing and Taipei had become the fundamental elements shaping the relationship.

After Normalization, Contact Without Compromise

It did not take the mainland long to attempt to capitalize on the normalization of Sino-American relations by enticing Taiwan. On January 1, 1979, the PRC announced that the intermittent shelling of the offshore islands would cease and it called for talks as well as direct links across the strait in areas ranging from travel to shipping to sports exchanges. Over the next five years the mainland's leaders built on these proposals in a series of statements and interviews, laying out the fundamental outlines of the mainland policy toward Taiwan that remains in place today.

Sticking to the position taken since the 1950s, Deng Xiaoping and his colleagues maintained that there was only one China; that Taiwan was a province of the PRC under Beijing's sovereignty; and that while they would seek to achieve reunification by peaceful means, they would never abjure military means, which might be required under certain circumstances (e.g., a declaration of independence by Taiwan, the development of nuclear weapons or political instability on the island). The new element in the post-1978 initiatives was the concept of "one country, two systems." This concept explicitly stated that Taiwan's subordinate status in any reunification was a "nonnegotiable principle." However, it did pledge that the island, as a "special administrative region," would enjoy significant autonomy in regard to economic affairs, politics, culture and military affairs. Taiwan could even continue its foreign economic relations, although Beijing would represent all of China internationally.

Still reeling from the blow of derecognition and the insecurity it generated, the administration of Chiang Ching-kuo was in no mood to respond to these initiatives. Although foreign isolation stimulated democratization at home, in foreign policy it promoted a circle-the-wagons mentality that dictated a rigid posture toward the mainland. Amid constant reminders of the Communists' past perfidy, Taipei adhered to the policy of "three nos" enunciated by Chiang Ching-kuo—no talks, no compromise and no contact. At the time such an inflexible policy was not only consistent with the insecure mood on the island but it was also politically wise. It allayed the suspicions of both anti-KMT activists, who feared a secret deal with the mainland, and the anti-Communist old guard, who would hear of no compromises.

Ironically, it was in response to pressures from this old guard, as well as from the business community, that elements of flexibility were eventually introduced into mainland policy. This pressure stemmed from the desire of many on Taiwan (including KMT soldiers) to visit relatives on the mainland. In July 1987 the government announced that applications to visit Hong Kong and Macao (entrepôts to the mainland) would be accepted; in November the new policy was extended to travel to the mainland. At about the same time citizens of Taiwan were allowed to take currency out of the country, and indirect trade with the mainland was permitted. These changes established the basis for economic ties with the PRC.

Mainland-Taiwan Economic Relations Burgeon

In the years after 1988 (when Chiang died), economic relations between the mainland and Taiwan expanded beyond all expectations. There were solid economic reasons for this as Taiwanese producers, facing rising labor costs, sought new sources of labor and new markets on the mainland. Although the government sought to channel overseas investment in other directions, particularly to Southeast Asia, the attraction of a common language, culture and in some cases relatives was too strong. By the end of 1995, Taiwan's contracted investment in the mainland stood at U.S. $29.4 billion, representing roughly 40 percent of the island's foreign investment in that year. Although the early pattern of investment was for labor-intensive industries to relocate to southern mainland provinces, by 1994 investment was expanding to places such as Shanghai and Jiangsu province, with electronics and food products leading the way and factories being built to produce materials such as plastics and resins. Meanwhile two-way trade grew from U.S. $2.7 million in 1988 to U.S. $15 billion in 1993. In 1996 it reached U.S. $ 22.2 billion or 10 percent of total foreign trade (a concern for some on the island), with Taiwan enjoying a favorable balance of nearly U.S. $16 billion due in large part to the export of raw materials, component parts, synthetic fibers and production goods to be used by entrepreneurs on the mainland.

Even more remarkable than the size of Taiwan's economic presence on the mainland were the circumstances under which it expanded. These years saw little progress—and even occasional crises—in the relations between the PRC and Taiwan. The lack of direct shipping links necessitated transshipment through Hong Kong; companies wishing to invest in large projects on the mainland needed Taipei's approval; and finally, while the mainland promised special privileges and protection to companies from Taiwan, all nevertheless had to face the uncertain investment environment there. Still, the business people came, and they were joined by cultural delegations, journalists (as of December 1996, Taiwanese correspondents had made more than 5,000 trips to the mainland), sports teams and more than 6 million ordinary tourists from Taiwan.

What became known as mainland fever in the early 1990s is best seen as part of the broader mobilization of society that occurred during the late 1980s. Like environmental groups, church groups and labor organizations, the business community was showing that it would no longer be dominated by the Kuomintang. It was shaping policy toward the mainland by creating *faits accomplis*, which the government eventually was forced to ratify through changed legislation. By 1990–91, in an effort to bring this "anarchical" situation under control, the government on Taiwan created programmatic and institutional structures that it hoped would direct mainland relations.

The first steps were the drafting, in February 1991, of "Guidelines for National Unification," by the newly formed National Unification Council under the president's office, and a presidential decree, in May, ending the state of national emergency occasioned by the "Communist Rebellion." The latter declaration created the conditions for further democratization and sent a conciliatory signal to the PRC. The guidelines were more programmatic. Stating that the unification of China was "the common wish of the Chinese people at home and abroad," they proceeded to lay out conditions and something of a timetable for reaching that goal. Two conditions were central: that unification "respect the rights and interests of the people in the Taiwan area" and that it result in a "democratic, free and equitably prosperous China." The timetable projected three stages in the unification process. In the short term (present phase), people-to-people exchanges would take place, hostility would end (including the mainland's opposition to Taiwan playing a global role), "democracy and rule of law...[would] be implemented on the mainland," and "mutual trust and cooperation" developed. Should these goals be achieved, relations would enter an intermediate stage characterized by "direct postal, transport and commercial links," official contacts and mutual assistance in "taking part in international organizations and activities." This having been accomplished, in a final phase unification negotiations would begin.

Walking a Diplomatic Tightrope

The guidelines were a thinly veiled attempt to satisfy the competing demands of domestic and external policies. They were intended to assure Beijing that the commitment to ultimate unification was unshaken. The operative word was "ultimate." The process envisioned would obviously be a slow

Danziger©The Christian Science Publishing Society.
All rights reserved. Reprinted with permission.

one necessitating a virtual liberal democratic revolution on the mainland before even the intermediate stage could be entered. People-to-people relations would obviously be the extent of mainland-Taiwan relations for some time. At home, the establishment of seemingly unattainable conditions for unification and the encouragement of nonofficial contacts were clearly intended to satisfy two constituencies: those pressing for distance, or even independence, from the mainland and the business community, which was concerned that cross-strait politics might interfere with trade and investment.

Two New Institutions

In order to manage relations with the mainland, two important bureaucracies were established in 1991. The first was the Straits Exchange Foundation (SEF), which was charged with making any necessary contacts with the mainland. Consistent with the requirement that all contacts be unofficial, this body was nominally a private foundation. The SEF was actually semiofficial, however, as it had government officials on its board and received government funding. In addition, it was closely supervised by the second newly formed bureaucracy, the Mainland Affairs Council (MAC), a cabinet-level body charged with coordinating mainland policy. In theory the National Unification Council would draw general guidelines; the MAC would translate these into policy guiding all economic ties, cultural exchanges and "nonofficial" contacts with mainland officials; and the SEF would be the "white glove" organization that would meet with those officials.

Yet even these cautious steps were viewed with suspicion by those who believed that despite the leadership of Taiwan-born Lee Teng-hui, the KMT might be promoting unification with the mainland. It was these expressions of suspicion, together with the popular sentiment favoring distance from the mainland which they represented, that were the principal forces stimulating the simultaneous development in the early 1990s of a foreign policy known as pragmatic diplomacy or flexible diplomacy. This policy not only sought to expand the scope and visibility of Taiwan's "nonofficial" contacts. It also included dramatic new initiatives in other, more official areas, such as a bid to rejoin the UN and the expansion of formal diplomatic relations.

Combining new initiatives on mainland policy with pragmatic diplomacy was an astute political move intended to address a wide range of concerns within Taiwan. The old guard within the KMT was pleased with the evidence of Lee's continued commitment to the mainland; those seeking greater distance welcomed the talk of international recognition for Taiwan; and the business community generally greeted initiatives that would give the island greater global prominence and facilitate ties with the mainland. As a way of dealing with Taiwan's post-1979 status, the combination had some virtues as well, allowing the island to expand international contacts even as it sought to minimize mainland anger by retaining cross-strait contact and making pledges of future unification. The mainland might thus be kept at bay while Taiwan enjoyed the benefits of de facto independence. There was only one problem with this strategy: the deeply suspicious leadership in Beijing would not be that easily fooled. Over time it became clear that the mainland leadership believed that pragmatic diplomacy was, in fact, undermining progress toward reunification.

The mainland's initial response to Lee's 1991 policy and organizational initiatives was cautiously positive. In December 1991 the PRC established a counterpart organization to the SEF, the semiofficial Association for Relations Across the Straits (Arats). Although declared to be "a mass organization in the form of a corporate body," it was chaired by an influential former mayor of Shanghai, with a former foreign ministry official serving as secretary-general, and it operated under close party/state supervision. However, since neither it nor its "unofficial" counterpart on Taiwan was far removed from its respective government, politically sensitive issues intruded, making the settling of technical questions difficult.

After a rocky beginning, relations seemed by the end of 1992 to have taken a steadier tack. The SEF accepted an invitation from Arats to hold a meeting of the chairmen of the two bodies in Singapore. The event, held in April 1993, was billed as the highest level talks between the two sides since 1949. However, it accomplished very little of substance: a schedule was set for future SEF-Arats meetings and a few minor, purely technical documents were signed.

In the wake of the Singapore talks, relations between the two sides worsened. In the summer of 1993, the mainland came out with a strongly worded "White Paper" sharply condemning Lee Teng-hui's "pragmatic diplomacy." Beijing reserved the right to use force in settling the unification issue and expressed determination to oppose Taiwan's admission to the UN or any expanded "official relations" with countries recognizing Beijing. By early 1994, relations hit a post-1988 low when a group of Taiwanese tourists were murdered on the mainland, leading to a temporary slowdown of Taiwanese investment and expressions of outrage. The business community soon reconsidered its primary interest, however, and trade, tourism and investment resumed their vigorous growth.

Despite these economic trends, through the summer and fall of 1994 political relations between Taiwan and the mainland continued on their generally downward trajectory as the incompatibility of improved relations with the mainland and Taiwan's pragmatic diplomacy became apparent. Beijing regarded Lee and the KMT as insincere in their statements regarding unification, arguing that their real goal was the continuation of the status quo of separation from the mainland while economic benefits continued to flow into the island from relations across the strait.

Brief Upturn in Relations

By early 1995, momentum in the relationship seemed to have resumed. On Taiwan, a former minister of economic affairs, Vincent Siew, had been appointed head of the Mainland Affairs Council. Siew had long argued for closer economic ties with the mainland and announced upon his appointment that he would consider ways to facilitate shipping ties. In January, the general secretary of the Chinese Communist party, Jiang Zemin, unveiled an eight-point proposal which, while making no dramatic departures from previous statements, suggested the PRC's openness to broader negotiations. In April, Lee replied cautiously but with a suggestion of similar openness. It seemed that cross-strait relations were on the verge of moving in a more constructive direction. Plans were advancing for a second meeting of the chairmen of the Straits Exchange Foundation and the Association for Relations Across the Straits in July. Press reports suggested that the talks would be of a much wider scope than those in Singapore; Taiwan's representative stated that a "policy dialogue" might be begun on the proposals by Jiang and Lee. It was at this juncture that the announcement came that Lee Teng-hui would be visiting Cornell University.

The trip and Lee's speech incensed the leadership in Beijing. They charged that the visit "destroyed" relations, and the trend in Taiwan-mainland relations was suddenly reversed. For Lee Teng-hui, about to face his first election challenge within less than a year, the visit would elevate his own position. However, the trip struck two sensitive chords on the mainland. It confirmed suspicions that Lee's diplomacy was really aimed at giving substance to Taiwan's independence by fostering wider "official" relations and it rekindled suspicions regarding American meddling in the Taiwan question.

These perceptions arose at a time of uncertain bilateral relations between Washington and the PRC during the first years of the Clinton Administration. Beijing's concerns about America's role as a single superpower were matched by Washington's misgivings regarding the implications of a rapidly emerging China. Differences on economic ties, intellectual-property rights, arms sales and human rights led Sino-American relations to lurch from conflict to conflict. The two nations were struggling to find a basis for the relationship that would repair the damage done by Tiananmen and replace the shared anti-Soviet entente of the 1970s and 1980s.

Lee's admission to the United States despite earlier Administration assurances that this would never be allowed suggested foreign interference in the Taiwan question and was bitterly denounced in the PRC. After some hesitation, the SEF-Arats summer talks were canceled, protests were made to Washington and the mainland conducted military exercises to express its irritation. Although the real target of Beijing's unhappiness was the United States, these activities also warned Taiwan to limit its pragmatic diplomacy.

Mainland relations with Taiwan worsened during the rest of 1995. As had been the case in the past, trade and investment continued to grow, but cross-strait dialogue virtually ended and was replaced by angry and defiant rhetoric. There was evidence that domestic politics were becoming a factor in the PRC. It was rumored that Lee's U.S. visit had discredited Communist party leader Jiang Zemin and his more moderate Taiwan policy while increasing the influence of those, particularly in the military, who were dissatisfied with the slow progress toward reunification. For the remainder of the year Beijing bitterly denounced those who pursued independence in both "word and deed," an obvious reference to both the DPP and Lee Teng-hui.

In Taiwan, domestic politics also certainly figured heavily in mainland relations, as Lee built on his diplomatic coup to substantiate his posture as a president who could stand up to the mainland and give Taiwan the international stature it deserved. The preelection environment was not a time to be conciliatory toward the mainland or pull back on pragmatic diplomacy. On the eve of the elections, the PRC raised the ante, resorting to intimidation through missile tests close to the Taiwan coast and military exercises, including amphibious training, on the coast of the mainland. As has been noted, this mainland intimidation backfired, as many people apparently voted for Lee in defiance of the mainland and with the perception that he was most likely to maintain the status quo (i.e., separation) in mainland relations.

Still, the months of mainland threats had an effect on the

One week before Taiwan's first direct presidential elections, Taiwanese protesters denounce China's military exercises near the Taiwan Strait by parading an effigy of Chinese President Jiang Zemin holding an M-11 missile.

leaders in Taipei. The crisis had had a serious impact on the economy and the public was uneasy. Without retreating from their fundamental stance, they did mute some of the rhetoric that Beijing found most objectionable, and they continued to express readiness to reopen the cross-strait dialogue suspended in the summer of 1995. At his inauguration in May 1996, Lee Teng-hui expressed his willingness to make a "journey of peace" to Beijing to meet with PRC officials. The missiles of March seemed to have had a sobering effect.

Even so, pragmatic diplomacy continued, despite the blow dealt when South Africa, the last remaining important nation maintaining formal relations with Taiwan, announced in late 1996 that it would shift its recognition to Beijing. With the vice president and the foreign minister visiting Ukraine and Belgium, "unofficial relations" expanding with a wide range of countries and yet another bid being made to enter the UN, it seemed that the newly elected administration would make few radical departures from earlier policies.

The confrontation of March had, for the first time since the mid-1980s, put Taiwan back at center stage in Sino-American relations. It seemed to crystallize the debate regarding the formulation of an appropriate policy toward a PRC that was rapidly becoming a major power in Asia. Those who sought a tougher line were gratified by strong rhetoric from the Clinton Administration (Beijing's actions were characterized as "reckless") and the dispatching of two aircraft-carrier battle groups to the Taiwan Strait in the largest American naval deployment in Asia since the Vietnam War, even if they were only to patrol. On the other hand, after the crisis, some of Taiwan's supporters, particularly in Congress, taken aback by the strength of the mainland reaction, moved to moderate the U.S. position as well as that of Taiwan.

Throughout the confrontation, however, it was clear that while Washington sought to stick by its position regarding peaceful unification, the extent of its commitment to Taiwan was unclear. Indeed, the Administration kept U.S. policy ambiguous intentionally. Ambiguity served two purposes: it was meant to moderate Taipei's policies by placing the island on notice that it could not expect unconditional support in the event of a conflict with the mainland, and it was designed to warn Beijing of possible consequences if it used force. In these respects the policy seemed to have succeeded.

As the cross-strait relationship approaches its fiftieth year— and the Chinese civil war, its seventieth—not only do the fundamental issues remain unresolved, but both sides seem to be drifting further apart. The leaders of the PRC remain insistent on claiming the rightful fruits of their 1949 victory, retaking territory belonging to the mainland and ending what they see as foreign intervention in a domestic matter. On Taiwan, much of the population seems far removed from the mainland experience and satisfied with their current status, while the government moves further away from the old KMT. Talk of unification seems more a way of keeping the mainland satisfied—and at arm's length.

Still, an impasse is not a solution. It not only complicates future economic development and overshadows the entire democratization process but it also seriously limits any improvement in the island's international status.

4

Conclusion

I N HIS year-end speech, Lee Teng-hui declared that 1996 had been "the most fruitful and brilliant year in the ROC's history." He was, of course, referring primarily to the accomplishments in the political realm, where he became the first popularly elected president in Chinese history. However, in retrospect, it seems that 1996 will be known less for political accomplishments than for the important and complex turning points that Taiwan reached in that year.

Restructuring and Realigning the Political System

Since 1988, Taiwan's constitutional reform has proceeded in an incremental and piecemeal fashion. However, by 1996, constitutional flexibility seemed to be reaching its limits. Incremental change had created political ambiguities and problems that needed to be resolved if progress were to be continued.

In the first place, the election of a "national government" by the people of Taiwan raised questions about the administrative duplication and expense caused by the continued existence of a provincial government. There was also the question of the fundamental nature of the government. It is clear that the president's office has gained considerable power. Yet the government has not been a presidential one similar to that of France or the United States. The premier and the Executive Yuan which he heads have been responsible for initiating legislation and managing the everyday affairs of government in ways that suggest a parliamentary-cabinet system such as that in Britain. Yet the premier has been chosen by the president, and although he can receive a vote of no confidence from the Legislative Yuan forcing him to resign, new parliamentary elections cannot be called as would be the case in Britain. The result of this muddle, then, has been not simply a dangerously unclear division of power between the president and the premier. There exists the possibility (very real, given the slim KMT majority) of a situation in which the legislature rejects one premier after another without fear of dissolution, leading to either governmental gridlock or a shaky coalition government.

In the spring of 1996, Lee Teng-hui spoke of the need to deal with these issues, and December 23–28 of that year a National Development Conference was held, which brought together representatives of the major parties as well as invited academics and others. Its results were remarkable both for what they proposed and for the fact that they were the product of joint efforts by the KMT and its longtime opponent, the DPP; the New party representatives walked out.

The proposed changes increased the power of the president by giving him the authority to appoint the premier without legislative approval and to dissolve the legislature. The power of the Legislative Yuan was increased by allowing it to cast no-confidence votes, to hold committee hearings, to investigate government offices and to impeach the president and vice president. There were proposals to reduce the importance and size of the provincial government, reorganize and lessen the power of the National Assembly, change the size and method of election of the Legislative Yuan and, in an attempt to reduce corruption at the local level, appoint town and village officials rather than elect them.

Party Alignments Changing

Despite the fact that the proposals have the support of the island's two leading parties, they still have to clear a number of hurdles before they become the law of the land. Not the least of these obstacles is the fact that there have been rumblings of dissatisfaction and shifting positions among the members of the National Assembly (the body that must amend the constitution!). Constitutional reform has thus become enmeshed in partisan politics. To complicate matters even further, such entanglement is occurring at a time when party alignments in Taiwan seem to be undergoing a basic change occasioned by the elections of 1995–96.

While it has adjusted to the demands of mass-based electoral politics, the KMT carries traces of its Leninist past. The party, chaired by the president, makes major appointments and crucial decisions behind closed doors, shielded from public scrutiny. Furthermore, the KMT still benefits from its past control of the island's media and from its considerable wealth derived from extensive local and global investments. Its longevity and business interests have inevitably raised charges of political and economic corruption that continue to haunt the party. Finally, and most importantly, the KMT has yet to address the issue of a transition to the post-Lee Teng-hui era.

The Democratic Progressive party's fundamental problem is that much of its original program has become either irrelevant or irresponsible in the eyes of the voters. Lee Teng-hui's pragmatic diplomacy and campaign to enter the UN co-opted DPP foreign policy planks. Calls for ethnic equality seem outdated at a time when mainlander/islander tensions have been reduced by an official KMT investigation into, and then an apology and reparations for, the 2/28 Incident; the passing of time and cultural intermingling of the two groups of Chinese; and the fact that most national officials are now islanders by origin. The same is true of earlier calls for democratization and a lessening of one-party rule. Finally, the call for Taiwanese independence and maintaining distance from the mainland has alienated business people, who want greater contact with the mainland, and many other citizens who fear that the island's security is threatened by outright calls for a separate nation.

After its disappointing showing in the March 1996 elections, the DPP began a process of soul-searching. Its chairman and longtime leader, Shih Ming-teh, resigned. Its unsuccessful presidential candidate, Peng Ming-min, gave his support to a splinter organization promoting independence, which in December formed the National Construction party, a party of independence (which Peng did not join). The DPP appeared to be succumbing to its old problem of factionalism. Finally, the coalition-like behavior at the National Development Conference and the agreement with the KMT on a formula for presenting Taiwan as a sovereign entity equal to the PRC seemed to blur the lines between the DPP and its bitter foe of the last decade. At present, many of its members are looking for new issues that will create a viable opposition party with a platform capable of inspiring a larger share of the population.

Finally, there is the New party. The promise of this party has also proven to be its essential weakness. Its following among the young and emerging middle class in the urban areas (many of whom are islanders), as well as among old-time KMT elements, appears to make it a perfect representative of the new, united Taiwan. Yet these constituencies are also the basis of its fundamental weakness. Not only do they expose an underlying fault line that threatens party unity but behind the rhetoric of a call for clean government lies a largely negative platform: the party is united simply around the issue of opposition to what the KMT government has become under Lee Teng-hui. This fact, coupled with continued suspicions regarding the party's unificationist orientation, has undoubtedly been an important reason for the leveling off of its support.

For the immediate future, Taiwan's domestic environment will remain unsettled. Although agreement seems to have been reached on a plan for fundamental constitutional reform, the process has just begun. A realignment of the two major parties has created a coalition capable of promoting an ambitious legislative program, but how this will work in practice remains to be seen. Elections for local offices will take place in the fall of 1997; it is unclear what impact the heat of electoral politics will have on that coalition.

There is also some question as to whether the present government and party structure can address fundamental problems facing the island. Despite the prominence of cross-strait relations in party politics, most Taiwanese are focused on more mundane domestic issues. Environmental protection, an early stimulant of popular participation, remains an important issue. However, the problems of crime and political corruption dominate. These were brought home to many in late 1996 when a district magistrate and seven associates died in a gangland-style killing and a DPP women's-rights activist was found raped and murdered. It is not surprising that Premier Lien Chan announced that 1997 will be an anticrime year.

The Economy at a Crossroads

As 1996 came to an end, there was good reason for uneasiness regarding the direction and pace of economic growth. There was, of course, some good news. Exports were continuing to grow (they reached a record high of U.S. $116 billion in 1996) and Taiwan was taking its place as a major producer and exporter of high-tech goods (in 1996 technology-intensive goods represented 61 percent of exports). This sector of the economy was showing signs of success as foreign partners were joining the island's firms in their quest to develop new product lines. Moreover, the effort to open the economy to foreign business and banking was beginning to pay off as increasing numbers of corporations sought to establish operations on the island. Major companies, including Citibank, Federal Express and Philips Electronics, announced plans to expand their Taiwan operations. Finally, at the end of the year, foreign-exchange holdings remained strong.

Signs of economic problems and looming challenges, however, overshadowed these favorable developments. Taiwan's export growth has slowed as compared with past years and overall economic growth has fallen short of expectations. In 1996 unemployment hit a 10-year high. Factory closings are, in part, a consequence of the changing shape of Taiwan's economy. The service sector is growing and the manufacturing sector is shifting away from labor-intensive goods. Rising unemployment is also related to the liberalization of the economy that has taken place over the past few years. A fundamental requirement for joining the World Trade Organization and developing the island as a regional operations hub is greater integration into the global economy. This requires a lowering of the barriers that have kept domestic investors on the island and potential foreign investors off. Mainstays of the economic miracle, such as discriminatory tariffs, government manufacturing monopolies and central control of the financial and banking system, will have to be phased out.

This amounts to a virtual economic revolution. The size of the government bureaucracies will be reduced; those administrators who remain will have to develop wholly different modes of behavior; and innumerable laws will need to be passed in order to regulate the very changed economy that will emerge. Bureaucrats will not be the only ones whose jobs will be threatened. Workers in factories that are unable to compete with foreign-held factories will become unemployed, as will many in agriculture, telecommunications and automobile manufacturing that have benefited from tariff protection or monopoly status. As the government has proceeded with discussions on membership in the World Trade Organization, Taiwan's negotiators and potentially affected groups at home have shown increasing concern regarding the ramifications of globalization. Still, recognizing the political and economic benefits that membership will bring, Taiwan continues to press for admission.

In the past Taiwan's authoritarian government was able to move the economy in new directions because of its relative insulation from political pressures from opposing groups or bureaucracies. Today the situation is more complicated. Democratization has meant that government can no longer stand above societal forces but must respond to them. Given the wide impact that globalization of the economy and

Taiwan's development as an operations center will have on farmers, business people and workers, one can only expect that the course of the transformation will be complicated by considerable political strife.

There is also uncertainty regarding the extent and pace of implementing the new policies. Progress has been slow in getting new regulations in place. The shifting structure of government and the inertia of bureaucrats, who are either committed to old policies or unable to operate in the new, liberalized environment, raise questions both in Taiwan and abroad about the likely success of the latest course change in economic policies.

A welcoming and receptive international environment will also be crucial to the success of the island's economic transition. For an entity that maintains diplomatic ties with relatively few small nations and is excluded from many major international organizations, Taiwan has done remarkably well. It has successfully concluded WTO-related talks with a number of countries and took part in the organization's first ministerial conference in Singapore in mid-December 1996. Taiwan remains an active force in the international economy; its products can be found almost anywhere on the globe.

Yet Taiwan's economic efforts continue to be plagued by cross-strait tensions. While many trading partners value their relationship with Taiwan, they are also looking toward even larger economic opportunities on the mainland. They are reluctant to do anything that might harm these future prospects or alienate a country with considerable economic influence. Because Beijing has no qualms about using this leverage, these sensitivities have been a major factor in slowing Taiwan's entrance into major international economic organizations. Most important, many nations seem prepared to accept Beijing's demand that the island be admitted to the WTO only after the PRC has been admitted. The result is that this centerpiece of Taiwan's plans for the future is being held hostage to a factor beyond its control: sufficient reforms on the mainland to gain global acceptance of its WTO application.

The mainland can affect the island's future economic development even more adversely in other ways. Taiwanese officials' frequently expressed fear that the extent of the island's trade with, and investments on, the mainland will result in dependency and make it subject to blackmail is probably overstated, but the fact is that a radical change in relations would have a significant impact on the economies of both the island and the mainland. Moreover, should tensions with the mainland develop into a confrontation similar to the one in the spring of 1996, foreign interest in Taiwan as a regional hub would most likely disappear, and investment in the island's economy would become less attractive. In sum, whether Taipei's leaders like it or not, successful economic reform depends on more than a temporary truce in cross-strait relations. The road to reform truly goes through Beijing.

Cross-Strait Relations at an Impasse

The cumulative impact of Lee Teng-hui's visit to Cornell University and the presidential elections that followed less than a year later was to freeze the "semiofficial" contacts that had been developing between the mainland and Taiwan. Cross-strait rhetoric became ever more bitter, seeming to lock both sides into positions that would allow little compromise.

Since June 1995 the mainland has made moves in the international arena to thwart any continuation, let alone expansion, of the core element in Lee Teng-hui's foreign policy: pragmatic diplomacy. Over the past two years the mainland press has dismissed Lee's continued commitment to unification as a rhetorical cover for independence. It has also attacked his character, suggesting that he is a traitor who thinks more like a subject of the Japanese emperor than a Chinese citizen. With regard to his foreign policy, Beijing has insisted that attempts to enter the UN end, that visits by Taiwanese leaders to countries with which China has relations cease and that the United States stop intervening in cross-strait relations. Most important, Taiwan must accept the PRC's definition of the principle of "one China," in which the island is no more than a province of the People's Republic of China.

By early 1997 it was apparent that the mainland was doing more than talking; the PRC was actively directing its foreign policy toward reducing Taiwan's international visibility. At the UN the mainland argued vigorously and successfully against Taiwan's admission and, in its first use of a Security Council veto, blocked the dispatch of peacekeeping troops to Guatemala until the Guatemalan government agreed to drop its support of the effort by Taiwan to have the issue of its membership included on the UN agenda. Finally, taking a leaf from Taiwan's book, Beijing has sought to establish "unofficial" trade offices in countries maintaining diplomatic relations with Taipei.

In response, Taiwan has given little ground. It has continued to refer to itself as the Republic of China on Taiwan (a formula condemned by the mainland) and to declare itself a sovereign state. Taipei has stated publicly that it will continue pragmatic diplomacy, even arguing that from Taiwan's perspective such diplomacy is more important than relations with the mainland. Taipei has also not halted its unsuccessful campaign to enter the UN. Finally, the island has been searching for ways to frustrate attempts to isolate it. Ties with countries with which it maintains relations have been carefully cultivated by visits and promises of aid, unofficial trade relations have been expanded, and high-ranking officials from Taiwan have made unannounced trips to countries such as Belgium, Ukraine and Jordan (all of which have official relations with the mainland).

In such an atmosphere of mutual recrimination and cat-and-mouse international politics, it is not surprising that the "unofficial" dialogue begun in 1991 has been frozen. However, this does not mean that cross-strait relations have stalled. They have continued and in some respects even expanded. Although the tensions of the past two years have caused considerable fluctuation in trade and investment, there have been only slight signs of a slowdown. According to Taiwan's Board of Foreign Trade, two-way trade across the strait in 1996 increased approximately 6 percent over 1995. Investment, on the other hand, slowed because of political uncertainty and pressure from Lee Teng-hui.

There have also been signs of expansion in the institutions that manage unofficial relations, with delegations of legislators, party and local officials visiting the mainland. Of particular note is the increasing prominence of commercial delegations, which have always played a significant role in cross-strait relations but seem to be growing in importance. Indeed, although officials were in attendance, it was a meeting of shipping associations held in Hong Kong in January 1997 that hammered out an agreement regarding direct sea trade links across the Taiwan Strait. Although this agreement has not addressed all issues or eliminated all problems with such shipping (in particular, complex regulations on the Taiwan side), it has begun a process that has been welcomed by much of the business community on the island.

Some Progress on Issue of Hong Kong's Return

According to unilateral announcements on both sides, significant progress was made toward resolving issues related to Hong Kong's return to China in 1997. The former British colony is an essential entrepôt and headquarters for Taiwan's trade with the mainland. Although there has been talk of seeking other locations (Okinawa, for example), Taiwan would like to maintain its trading position in Hong Kong. The PRC, seeking to protect its economic interests, has not been uncooperative. In June 1996, clearly with the mainland's approval, an agreement was struck on air travel from Taiwan to straddle the handover of the colony in July 1997. Soon afterward, Beijing announced that Taiwan's existing Hong Kong offices could stay provided they abided by the "one-China principle" and obeyed the law. To be sure, there are limits to these kinds of indirect agreements and it is by no means clear how Beijing will interpret the conditions it has placed on Taiwan, but some mutual adjustment has begun.

It is uncertain whether these less-visible developments will change the basic structure of cross-strait relations. Despite pressures from the business community, there is reluctance in Taipei to expand economic ties. Taiwan's repeated calls for new talks—

and even an unprecedented willingness to discuss political or policy questions that had been outside the scope of earlier dialogues—occur against a background of inflexibility on basic issues. Lee and his colleagues show little sign of being ready to compromise their positions on such issues as the sovereignty of Taiwan or the need for the mainland to renounce the use of force and to ease its attempts to isolate Taiwan internationally.

More importantly, the mainland issue has become thoroughly and irretrievably enmeshed in Taiwan's domestic politics. In contrast to many earlier studies, this discussion has devoted little attention to the question of mainlander/islander relations on Taiwan. Over the years, not only has there been a process of mutual acculturation and adjustment, but a political modus vivendi has been reached. Although ethnicity is still a factor in party support (for example, most DPP supporters are still islanders rather than mainlanders), the KMT's evolution and stance on relations with the mainland have done much to bridge the gap. It is precisely for this reason that it is unlikely that Taiwan will fundamentally change its policy on the mainland in the near future. The position that Lee has called "a golden mean" between proclaimed independence and accelerated unification is a key element in the island's unity and the KMT's continued success. It is not likely to be abandoned very soon.

The fact that Taiwan's approach is so fraught with distrust and so driven by domestic politics is an obstacle to any meaningful expansion of the informal relations of the past two years. Indeed, one might argue that the specific intent of Taiwan's pursuit of trade and contacts with the mainland has been to assure that it not lead to any broader relationship. Taipei has intended that such contacts maintain the illusion of forward motion in order to satisfy an expansive business community and keep the mainland at bay until such time as conditions improve. The essence of Taiwan's policy toward the mainland is to buy time.

The problem is that an increasingly impatient and cynical Beijing leadership has clearly caught on to this strategy and has become more and more insistent on deeds, not words. Maintaining that Taipei's provocative diplomatic behavior has ruined the "atmosphere" for cross-strait talks, the mainland has stuck to its demands for a change in Taiwan's posture. However, there are also signs that the mainland is stepping up its earlier policy of seeking to use popular pressure (specifically from the business community) to effect a change in Taiwan's basic policy. Beijing's assertions that it has "faith in the people" and that those who promote reunification will be remembered in Chinese history, coupled with its aggressive courting of Taiwanese business, suggest that Lee Teng-hui's concern about the mainland's manipulation of business ties may not be entirely unfounded.

The PRC's Priorities

It is also possible that this tack reflects a more fundamental element in the PRC's policy toward Taiwan: the desire to put the island issue on the back burner for the near future. This was suggested in early 1997 in a series of reports on recent mainland meetings published by usually reliable Hong Kong sources. It was noted that despite pressure from the military, the leadership in Beijing had decided for the next few years the focus would be on blunting any expansion of Taiwan's pragmatic diplomacy, securing a smooth transition in Hong Kong, improving relations with Japan and South Korea and selecting a new leadership for the post-Deng Xiaoping era.

Still, this policy direction is by no means fixed. Britain's return of Hong Kong to the PRC reflects this uncertainty. If the transition goes well and the PRC leadership keeps its pledge of broad autonomy for Hong Kong, then the pressure will increase on Taiwan to settle its differences with the mainland. If tensions develop between the Hong Kong public and the PRC, then intervention in the former colony's affairs will increase. Under these circumstances a mainland leadership impatient with negotiations and suspicious of foreign meddling may well increase the pressure on Taiwan. Such a hardening in Beijing's posture would undoubtedly both affect—and be reflected by—the Deng succession following his death on February 19, 1997. The Taiwan issue is one on which few aspiring leaders in the PRC can afford to appear soft. Domestic political pressures on the mainland, as on Taiwan, allow little flexibility in making policy.

It is possible that such a turn of events might lead to a military confrontation more serious than that of 1996. Such a solution to the cross-strait crisis has long weighed heavily on the minds of Taiwan's people. In the summer of 1994, a book outlining a successful invasion of the island was a best-seller there. Most analysts believe that with the infusion of American and French arms and the development of an indigenous production capacity, Taiwan has the capability to resist successfully a full-scale invasion from the mainland during the next decade. More problematic, however, are Taiwan's options at the other end of the coercive scale: the imposition of a blockade by the mainland's navy or the firing of missiles, as was the case in 1996, to intimidate the island or to deter it from pursuing what the mainland considers to be an unfriendly policy. For an island dependent on foreign commerce, either of these scenarios would be dangerous.

Yet, even if one assumes that the policy pursued by the PRC since 1995 continues, the future challenges for Taiwan will still be difficult. It is clear that the leadership in Beijing has formulated a policy that will curtail the island's quest for de facto independence. Globally, the PRC will seek to challenge attempts by Taiwan to expand its political relations both with international organizations and individual countries, while it seeks to isolate the island by improving relations with Japan and the United States. If the PRC remains stable and experiences continued economic growth, its international leverage will surely increase.

And so one must not underestimate the ambiguous nature of any calm in relations across the strait. On the one hand, both sides remain locked in fundamentally irreconcilable positions, their policies driven by domestic politics toward intransigence rather than compromise. For the near future, diplomatic skill, restraint and patience—qualities not found in abundance on either the mainland or Taiwan—will be needed to avoid sudden crises. Yet, on the other, it is also possible that more subtle policies might prevail which, although posing serious challenges to Taiwan's present strategies, could maintain the peace. Although it seems unlikely at the present, this peace, accompanied by policy changes on both sides of the strait, could provide the context for a mutually acceptable agreement.

U.S. Policy and Future Options

American policymakers also face a complex array of challenges. Undoubtedly, many in Washington would privately yearn for a return to the less complicated period before Lee's trip to the United States. However, that seems unlikely. America's public position is that it has no intention of pursuing a "two-China" or "one-China, one-Taiwan" policy, that the issue is for the two sides to settle between themselves and that the United States will accept any settlement as long as it is peaceful. The policy is inherently contradictory, for while Washington seeks to step back and allow the two sides to settle the matter peacefully, it cannot actually do so. The commitment to peaceful resolution requires involvement, and that involvement could, if badly managed, trigger a crisis that would end in armed conflict rather than peaceful resolution. American stakes are such that the United States cannot afford to do nothing in the face of potential crisis, yet much of what it might do could worsen rather than improve the situation. Little wonder, then, that the fundamental U.S. posture has been characterized by ambiguity and that a high-ranking U.S. Defense Department official told Beijing that he didn't know what would happen in the event of cross-strait conflict.

The commitment to Taiwan is an amalgam of national interest, historical ties, legal obligation (albeit ambiguous), American values, economic interests and domestic politics. The historic ties are deep. As for the legal obligation (as spokesmen on the island have been quick to note), the Taiwan Relations Act of 1979, while setting no clear course of action in the event of cross-strait conflict, does make an unambiguous commitment to the security of Taiwan that to many observers amounts to a moral obligation to intervene. This moral commitment has been strengthened by the developments of the past decade in Taiwan. Political reform (often contrasted with developments on the mainland) and the increasing liberalization of the economy evoke considerable sympathy in the United States simply because they are congruent with America's fundamental values. Of course, economic development has done more than enhance moral affinities; it has helped to develop a growing commercial relationship with the United States.

Finally, domestic politics in the United States is, of course, a crucial factor. As past history has shown, lessening of backing for the island or perceived slighting of its officials has led to both the mobilization of Taiwan's champions (especially in Congress) and pressures for gestures of support, which have only further complicated relations with the PRC. Indeed, pro-Taiwan sentiment may well have increased in recent years. Some analysts have questioned whether the "one-China" formula of the past continues to be relevant given the changes on the island and the PRC's definition of the term to mean Taiwan's incorporation into a China ruled from Beijing. Moreover, voices of concern have been raised in Washington warning of the danger to American global interests of a resurgent PRC emerging in Asia. Taiwan, it has been argued, is one of the places where the United States might draw a "line in the sand" and enhance the credibility of its commitment to stability in the region.

With regard to the PRC, the reasons for American involvement are also very compelling, if more complex. For more than a century the mystique of China has had a strong hold on the American people, conditioning what has been characterized as a love-hate relationship. In the years since 1949, cold-war bitterness turned to enthusiasm after the Nixon visit and then distrust in the wake of the Tiananmen demonstrations in 1989.

Still, there are compelling reasons why Sino-American relations must remain stable. The PRC is unquestionably an emerging power in Asia and the world. It is a nuclear power with a veto in the UN Security Council. Moreover, a host of crucial issues, from the environment to arms control to regional security to the international drug trade to the regional economic order, cannot be resolved without Beijing's participation. In addition, of course, as the fastest-growing and potentially the largest economy in the world, the PRC represents an enormous land of current and future opportunities for the American business community. At present, the United States is China's second-largest trading partner (nearly U.S. $64 billion), and American corporations are heavily invested in China. Many would argue that it is precisely such global economic ties that serve to restrain the PRC from jeopardizing its hard-won, post-Mao international status by provoking a military confrontation in the Taiwan Strait. In short, Washington does indeed have extremely important national security reasons to put the legacy of past distrust behind it and to move ahead with a vigorous policy of "constructive engagement" with the mainland.

It is thus easy to see why Washington might seek to cultivate relations with both sides of the strait and avoid taking a position on the central issues dividing them. Yet the deep antagonism between the two sides and their perception of the United States make such a policy extremely difficult to formulate. The quandary is obvious. America must cultivate common interests with the PRC without abandoning concern for Taiwan. Abandoning Taiwan might suggest to Beijing that it can settle the matter on its own terms or might push an isolated Taiwan to declare independence. Yet U.S.-Taiwan links must be such that they do not inadvertently create an illusion of support that would encourage further provocation of the mainland (or raise virtually unavoidable suspicions on the mainland that they are doing so).

In this Hobson's choice, Washington's policy has been to make it clear to the government in Taipei that support might not be forthcoming should it provoke the mainland by promoting Taiwan's sovereignty, and at the same time to persuade the PRC that it cannot expect the United States to stand by passively should it attempt a military solution. Neither side can consider that it has a blank check; each side is expected to think hard before provoking the other. The thrust of this policy is obvious: it seeks to maintain the peaceful status quo until conditions make it possible for both sides to come to an agreement. However, the immediate impact of such a policy is not only to ensure continued American involvement in a volatile situation, but to run the risk of increasing that volatility while placing the United States in a difficult position should conflict develop.

Specifically, should cross-strait relations drift toward the blockade scenario outlined above, U.S. policymakers would face some difficult choices. Would they act to break the blockade? Or would they stand by while Taiwan suffered through what would surely be an extended economic crisis? There is no clear answer. While many analysts think it unlikely that the United States would risk armed conflict, others find it equally unlikely that the United States could stand by and do nothing as the international media reported the slow strangulation of the island. It is a choice no Administration in Washington wants to face.

The nonconfrontational scenario outlined earlier, which would produce a settlement arrived at peacefully by the Chinese themselves, seems closer to the public stance taken by American policymakers. Yet even here there might be difficulties. Differing political groups in Taiwan could attempt to rally their backers in the United States, causing the island's political controversies to spill over into American politics. It is also possible that pressure could build for the United States to monitor any agreement, thus assuring Washington's continued involvement (undoubtedly unwanted by the PRC) and the consequences that might flow from that.

Thus, it appears that despite the inherent dangers and contradictions, the United States has little choice but to pursue its present policy that keeps it involved in a situation from which it seeks to withdraw. With cross-strait relations in an uncertain state, driven in great part by internal political forces and historical perceptions over which Washington has little control, that involvement must be managed carefully. Attention must be paid both to the limitations placed on American policy and the distrust of U.S. intentions harbored by both sides, lest such involvement spark the very crisis that it seeks to avoid.

Talking It Over

A Note for Students and Discussion Groups

This issue of the HEADLINE SERIES, like its predecessors, is published for every serious reader, specialized or not, who takes an interest in the subject. Many of our readers will be in classrooms, seminars or community discussion groups. Particularly with them in mind, we present below some discussion questions—suggested as a starting point only—and references for further reading.

Discussion Questions

Which aspects of the history of the Kuomintang and of the island of Taiwan do you think are most important in understanding contemporary Taiwanese politics? Which are less important?

What were the most important characteristics of the political system on Taiwan before 1988?

What has changed most as a result of democratization in Taiwan? What has changed the least? What still remains to be done?

What are the most important elements in Taiwan's "economic miracle"? In what ways is the future development of the island's economy likely to be similar to that of the past? In what ways might it be different?

How has American policy toward Taiwan changed since 1949? Are there any continuities?

How important have U.S.-Taiwan relations been in shaping the course of the U.S. relationship with the PRC? And vice versa?

Do you agree with the author's conclusions regarding the narrow range of options available to U.S. policymakers? What would you suggest as alternative policy options?

Reading List

Cheng, Tun-jen, Chi, Huang and Wu, Samuel S.G., eds., *Inherited Rivalry: Conflict Across the Taiwan Straits*. Boulder, CO, Lynne Rienner, 1995.

Chu, Yun-han, *Crafting Democracy in Taiwan*. Taipei, Taiwan, Institute for National Policy Research, 1992.

Clough, Ralph, *Island China*. Cambridge, MA, Harvard University Press, 1978.

———, *Reaching Across the Taiwan Strait: People to People Diplomacy*. Boulder, CO, Westview Press, 1993.

Feigenbaum, Evan A., *Change in Taiwan and Potential Adversity in the Strait*. Santa Monica, CA, Rand Corporation, 1995.

Gereffi, Gary, and Wyman, Donald, eds., *Manufacturing Miracles*. Princeton, NJ, Princeton University Press, 1991.

Gold, Thomas, *State and Society in the Taiwan Miracle*. Armonk, NY, Sharpe, 1986.

Harding, Harry, *A Fragile Relationship: The United States and China Since 1972*. Washington, DC, Brookings Institution, 1992.

Ross, Robert, *Negotiating Cooperation: The United States and China, 1969–1989*. Stanford, CA, Stanford University Press, 1995.

Schive, Chi, *Taiwan's Economic Role in East Asia*. Washington, DC, Center for Strategic and International Studies, 1995.

Simon, Denis, and Kau, Michael Y.M., eds., *Taiwan: Beyond the Economic Miracle*. Armonk, NY, Sharpe, 1992.

Tien, Hung-mao, ed., *Taiwan's Electoral Politics and Democratic Transition: Riding the Third Wave*. Armonk, NY, Sharpe, 1996.

Wade, Robert, *Governing the Market: Economic Theory and the Role of Government in East Asian Industrialization*. Princeton, NJ, Princeton University Press, 1990.